Pondering the Spade

Pondering the Spade

Discussing Important Convergences between
Archaeology and Old Testament Studies

David B. Schreiner

WIPF & STOCK · Eugene, Oregon

PONDERING THE SPADE
Discussing Important Convergences between Archaeology and Old Testament Studies

Wipf & Stock
An Imprint of Wipf and Stock Publishers
199 W. 8th Ave., Suite 3
Eugene, OR 97401

www.wipfandstock.com

PAPERBACK ISBN: 978-1-4982-9402-7
HARDCOVER ISBN: 978-1-4982-9404-1
EBOOK ISBN: 978-1-4982-9403-4

Manufactured in the U.S.A.

To my professors. I am forever grateful.

To my parents and brothers. You are some of my biggest fans.

To my daughters, Maddie, Bailey, and Lily.
I hope someday you'll realize I'm not that weird.

To Ginny. You make me a better man,
and I love you more each day.

To God be the glory . . .

"Read the land, live the book."

—Lawson G. Stone

Contents

Illustrations

Figure 01: The so-called Elisha Ostracon; photo courtesy of Lawson G. Stone, used by permission

Figure 02: The Rosetta Stone; Hans Hillewaert (CC BY-SA 4.0; https://up-load.wikimedia.org/wikipedia/commons/2/23/Rosetta_Stone.JPG)

Figure 03: The Apiary at Tel Rehov; photo courtesy of Lawson G. Stone, used by permission

Figure 04: Tablet of Zimri-Lim concerning the construction of an ice house; Louvre Museum (public domain; https://upload.wikimedia.org/wikipedia/commons/e/ee/Tablet_Zimri-Lim_Louvre_AO20161.jpg)

Figure 05: A Hallway of Zimri-Lim's palace; Gianfranco Gazzetti (CC BY-SA 4.0; https://commons.wikimedia.org/wiki/File:Mari_Palazzo_di_Zimri-Lim_-_GAR_-_7-03.jpg)

Figure 06: Clay liver models used in extispicy; Louvre Museum (public domain; https://commons.wikimedia.org/wiki/File:Divinatory_livers_Louvre_AO19837.jpg)

Figure 07: Tablet XI of the Gilgamesh Epic (public domain; https://commons.wikimedia.org/wiki/File:Literature_of_the_world_-_an_introductory_study_(1922)_(14782584192).jpg)

Figure 08: Palace at Ugarit; Ilario Di Nario (CC BY-SA 4.0; https://commons.wikimedia.org/wiki/File:Ugarit_Palazzo_Reale_-_GAR_-_1-01.jpg)

Figure 09: Baal the Canaanite Storm God; Louvre Museum (CC BY 3.0; https://commons.wikimedia.org/wiki/File:P1050759_Louvre_st%C3%A8le_du_Baal_au_foudre_rwk.JPG)

Historical Ages

(adapted from Amihai Mazar's *Archaeology of the Land of the Bible: 10,000–586 BCE* [The Anchor Bible Reference Library; New York: Doubleday, 1990])

Early Bronze Age c.a. 3300–2000 BCE
- EB I: c.a. 3300–3050 BCE
- EB II/III: 3050–c.a. 2300 BCE

Middle Bronze Age 2000–1550 BCE
- MB I: c.a. 2300–c.a. 2000 BCE
- MB II: c.a. 2000–1550 BCE

Late Bronze Age 1550–1200 BCE

Iron I 1200–1000 BCE
- Iron IA: 1200–1150 BCE
- Iron IB: 1150–1000 BCE

Iron II 1000–c.a. 550 BCE
- Iron IIA: 1000–925 BCE
- Iron IIB: 925–720 BCE
- Iron IIC: 720–c.a. 550 BCE

1

Introduction

I t was the hottest part of the day, and I was sitting in the shade at *Nir David*, a qibbutz near Tel Reḥov in the Jordan Valley. My friends and I were washing pottery, a daily and critical chore when on an excavation.[1] As I shot the breeze with Jason Jackson, I noticed something odd about the potsherd that I was washing. Set against the grayish background, there appeared to be red markings. I paused for a moment and then nudged Jason.

"What do you make of this, Jason?"

He was initially quiet, but then quickly responded, "I don't know."

We called one of the supervisors over, and as we waited in relative silence, we continued to ponder what we were looking at. Looking back on those initial moments, I know I realized what it was. I just kept quiet out of fear that my thoughts or words would somehow institute a jinx. My fears, however, were swept away and my initial impressions verified after about a second of my supervisor looking at the markings.

He squealed, "An inscription!"

Immediately, everyone else at the dig was clamoring for a look at the find. Pictures were taken, and after about five minutes, that ostracon was taken to the dig directors so that it could be catalogued, analyzed, and secured.

At that time, in 2008, I had just started my doctoral work at Asbury Theological Seminary, and one of my courses was in Northwest Semitic Inscriptions. Consequently, I recognized all the letters there were completely visible. And with a few moments of looking at one of the photographs, and

---

1. During excavation, a copious number of small broken pieces of pottery are gathered and deposited into buckets. The sherds are then tagged, taken to be washed, and subsequently analyzed so that they can serve as the backbone for the site's chronology. For an accessible discussion of the standard objectives and daily responsibilities, see John D. Currid, *Doing Archaeology in the Land of the Bible: A Basic Guide* (Grand Rapids: Baker Books, 1999).

after some discussion with my professors and colleagues, I was able to for-mulate what I thought it read. I would later find out that Director Amihai Mazar, along with Samuel Aḥituv, read the name "Elisha."[2] Of course, this produced several interesting responses, including a rather sensational one that was broadcast on the CBN website (see below).

Ostraca, or potsherds with writing on them, are one of the most im-portant finds for an archaeological dig. Indeed, the idea of potsherds with writing on them may seem mundane to many, but they can potentially provide a range of information that illuminates an ancient culture. For ex-ample, the Meṣad Ḥashavyahu ostraca give insight into how legal disputes were presented and, possibly, the place of biblical legislation in resolving them. Alternatively, ostraca may provide insight into the dynamics of lit-eracy. In fact, in recent memory, the place of ostraca in assessing literacy rates within ancient Israelite culture moved to the front of scholarly dis-course with the publication of a complex study in the *National Academies of Sciences* (abbr. *NAS*).

ostraca

2. Samuel Ahituv and Amihai Mazar, "The Inscriptions from Tel Rehov and their Contribution to the Study of Script and Writing during Iron Age IIA" in *"See I Will Bring a Scroll Recounting What Befell Me" (Is 40:8): Epigraphy and Daily Life from the Bible to the Talmud* (eds. Esther Eshel and Yigal Levin; Göttingen: Vandenhoeck & Ruprecht, 2014), 48–50.

In "Algorithmic Handwriting Analysis of Judah's Military Correspondence Sheds Light on Composition of Biblical Texts,"[3] a team of scholars and scientists subjected the Arad Ostraca, one of the most famous corpora of ostraca, to a sophisticated scheme of image processing and machine learning algorithms. Sampling sixteen sherds, the team found evidence for at least six different authors within the sample set. Thus, they concluded that there was a high degree of literacy within in certain circles of Judean society during the latter portion of Iron II. Furthermore, they projected that the composition of the Old Testament may have begun in earnest during this period.

The implications of this study are extraordinary, but not solely for reasons of dating the possible context of biblical composition. Indeed, it is interesting that this study openly entertains the possibility that the Old Testament's composition may have been an Iron Age phenomenon and not, say, a Persian one. Although, people like William Schniedewind and Christopher Rollston previously argued for such ideas.[4] No, the extraordinariness of the study exists in the nature of the investigation. It utilized innovative technologies, putting computers and computer programs front and center. Naturally then, one wonders is this study is indicative of a larger movement—the increasing importance of innovative technologies in analyzing material culture. This certainly seems to be the case, particularly since a few months after the publication of this article the directors of the Eli Levy Expedition at Ashkelon announced that they would subject the human remains of a Philistine cemetery to DNA profiling.[5] In another example, a team of scientists from the University of Kentucky were able to read the content of a miniature scroll that was essentially burnt to a crisp . . . they did it without even unrolling it![6]

3. Shira Faigenbaum-Golovin, *et. al.*, "Algorithmic Handwriting Analysis of Judah's Military Correspondence Sheds Light on Composition of Biblical Texts," *PNAS* 117.17 (2016): 4664–4669.

4. Christopher Rollston, *Writing and Literacy in the World of Ancient Israel: Epigraphic Evidence from the Iron Age* (Society of Biblical Literature: Archaeology and Biblical Studies 11. Atlanta: Society of Biblical Literature, 2010); William M. Schniedewind, *How the Bible Became a Book* (Cambridge: Cambridge University, 2004).

5. Nicholas St. Fleur, "Story of Philistines Could be Reshaped by Ancient Cemetery," *New York Times*, July 10, 2016 under "Science," http://www.nytimes.com/2016/07/11/science/possible-philistine-cemetery-discovered.html?smprod=nytcore-iphone&smid=nytcore-iphone-share (accessed Jan. 11, 2019).

6. Nicolas Wade, "Modern Technology Unlocks Secrets of Damaged Biblical Scroll," *New York Times*, Sept 21, 2016 under "Science," http://www.nytimes.com/2016/09/22/

Of course, studies like the one published by the *NAS* also have popular appeal. So, sensationalistic headlines followed. For example, "The Bible was Written Way Earlier Than We Thought, Mathematicians Suggest."[7] Or, "Ancient Sticky Notes Shift Secular Scholars Closer to Evangelicals on Bible's Age."[8] Yet there were more reserved headlines, such as "Does this Ancient Handwriting Prove the Bible's Age?"[9] In the end, however, it is critical that one must respond to such a study, and studies like them, responsibly and within the confines of their intentions. As I said in my response to the *NAS* study, the results imply that it is "more and more difficult not to put the composition of the majority of the Old Testament in the era of the monarchy, united or divided." Iron Age Israel exhibited the socio-political requirements necessary for literary production in antiquity, and this study by the *NAS* supports the claim.

Regardless of your position on the context of composition for the Old Testament, one cannot deny the increasing sophistication associated with archaeological research in general. As the study from the *NAS* shows, paleographic analysis, or the study of ancient systems of writing, is no longer solely a human endeavor. Consequently, this raises the question, "With its increasing sophistication, how will archaeology continue to inform Biblical Studies?" To answer, it is prudent to take a step back and consider how archaeology within Syria-Palestine developed *as a discipline*. It is within that framework that one can understand archaeology's relationship within Biblical Studies and the nature of its increasing sophistication.

science/ancient-sea-scrolls-bible.html?_r=0 (accessed Jan. 11, 2019).

7. BEC Crew, "The Bible was Written Way Earlier then We Thought, Mathematicians Suggest," *Science Alert*, April 12, 2016, http://www.sciencealert.com/the-bible-was-written-way-earlier-than-we-thought-mathematicians-discover (accessed Jan. 11, 2019).

8. Gordon Govier, "Ancient Sticky Notes Shift Secular Scholars Closer to Evangelicals on Bible's Age," *Christianity Today*, under "News," http://www.christianitytoday.com/ct/2016/april-web-only/ancient-sticky-notes-shift-secular-scholars-older-bible.html (accessed Sept 28, 2016).

9. Candida Moss, "Does this Handwriting Prove the Bible's Age?" *The Daily Beast*, http://www.thedailybeast.com/articles/2016/04/12/does-this-ancient-handwriting-prove-the-bible-s-age.html (accessed Jan. 11, 2019).

10. David B. Schreiner, "Potsherds, Computers, and the Composition of the Bible," Wesley Biblical Seminary, entry posted April 14, 2016, http://www.wbs.edu/2016/04/potsherds (accessed Jan. 11, 2019).

The Contours of Development

There have been many attempts to describe the historical contours of how archaeology relates to Biblical Studies. For example, John Currid divides the history into six phases,[11] but Ralph Hawkins divides the history into five.[12] Eric Cline describes the development around important figures in the field.[13] Indeed the history of the discipline is fascinating and worthy of comprehensive treatment.[14] Yet for the purposes here, only a basic description is necessary. Thus, I will harness the most important points made by those who have gone before me to describe a basic three-phase description. The first phase describes the development of archaeology in Syria-Palestine from its inception until the arrival of Sir Flinders Petrie. The second phase encompasses the pioneering work of Petrie and others through the heyday of "Biblical Archaeology." The final phase is also the present phase, which can be characterized by the rapid specialization and methodological development of the discipline. As one navigates the contours of the discipline, it will become clear that archaeology in Syria-Palestine has always been a field in search of more efficient, effective, and innovative methods.

Phase One: The Inception of Palestinian Exploration

Many credit Napoleon Bonaparte as the first person, very roughly speaking, to engage in near Eastern archaeology. As he trekked across the Mediterranean basin in search of fulfilling his grandiose vision of global conquest, he brought with him a team to record his findings.[15] Napoleon was apparently also keen on taking as many artifacts as possible. When he arrived in Egypt, one of the things taken was the Rosetta Stone, the famous black basalt monument honoring Ptolemy V.

11. John D. Currid, *Doing Archaeology*, 23–35.

12. Ralph Hawkins, "Biblical Archaeology" in *The Lexham Bible Dictionary* (ed. John D. Barry; Bellingham, WA: Lexham Press, 2016), Logos Bible Software.

13. Eric H. Cline, *Biblical Archaeology: A Very Short Introduction* (Oxford: Oxford University Press, 2009), 13–68.

14. For example, see P. R. Moorey, *A Century of Biblical Archaeology* (Louisville: Westminster John Knox, 1991).

15. Matthews contextualizes Bonaparte's effort in a context of competing nationalism across Europe. See "The West's Rediscovery of the Holy Land" in *The Old Testament in Archaeology and History* (eds. Jennie Ebling, *et. al.*; Waco: Baylor University Press, 2017), 92–99.

Manifesting three different languages, Greek, Egyptian Hieroglyphics, and Demotic, the decipherment of the text became the key to unlocking Egyptian Hieroglyphics—the language of perhaps the greatest culture of antiquity. So, make no mistake. The floodgates were open. Napoleon gave Europe its first taste of ancient Near Eastern society, and to this date, that appetite has yet to be satisfied.

The next great figure was Sir Edward Robinson. He arrived in the Middle East in the late 1830s with the intention of filling in the gaps created in his personal studies of biblical geography. He had a companion, Eli Smith, and together they traveled from Egypt to the northern reaches of what was ancient Israel. To identify sites, the two leaned heavily upon biblical descriptions and conversations with the local Arab population. Most importantly, they were not afraid to blaze new trails and consider sites that had yet to be considered. They meticulously measured distances and provided as much detail as possible. Ultimately, Robinson and Smith would publish *Biblical Researches in Palestine*, which amazingly has stood the test of time as it is still referenced by scholars in the field.[16] The Godfather of biblical geography produced a work to which all subsequent work is deeply indebted.

Robinson and Smith's work resonated loudly because by the end of the nineteenth century the region saw a boom in Western and European visitors. Along the way, these visitors took up the cause of becoming more acquainted with the Holy Land, and by the end of the nineteenth century several societies were founded with the expressed mandate to increase the investigation of the ancient Near East. *The Palestine Exploration Fund*, the *American Palestine Exploration Society*, the *Deutscher Verein zur Erforschung Palätinas*, and *École Biblique et Archéologique Française* were some of the more prominent examples. Moreover, this was the era that Charles Warren studied the Jerusalem's Temple Mount and its water source. Also, Lieutenants Claude Condor and H. H. Kitchener surveyed over 5000 square miles in the Trans-Jordan region. In each case, the task was relatively simple. Find as much significant material as possible and bring it home if the opportunity presented itself. Their methods were admittedly crude and materialistic.

Phase Two: The Rise of Systematic Archaeology

The first inklings of methodological precision began to creep into the picture with Sir Flinders Petrie.[17] His contributions to the development of archaeology in Syria-Palestine are predominately two-fold. First, Petrie was the first to formulate and incorporate an essential understanding of the tel. Tels are essentially mounds of occupation, and because cities were built on top of each other, a tel's history of occupation is preserved in the debris layers of the mound.[18] As for why a site was chosen for settlement, or why certain sites exhibited millennia of occupation? Sites were chosen for topographical, climatological, militaristic, and economic reasons. For example, sites that existed near a perennial water source, near a navigable trade route, or exhibited a posture that was easily defendable were preferred. Moreover, such sites were not quickly abandoned. Petrie understood this and realized

16. E. Robinson and E. Smith. *Biblical Researches in Palestine, and in the Adjacent Regions* (2 vols; Boston: Crocker and Brewster, 1856-1860). See Matthews, "The West's Rediscovery of the Holy Land," 105–07.

17. Cline recognizes this and calls Petrie the first "real biblical archaeologist." Cline, *Biblical Archaeology*, 21.

18. Currid, *Doing Archaeology*, 42.

that the debris layers within the tel were indicative of the site's occupational history. And if a tel could possibly illuminate the occupation of a site or even a region across time, then it's understandable why a tel quickly became the backbone of archaeological research within Syria-Palestine.

Petrie's realization, of course, demanded correlation between each layer of occupation. Therefore, a critical component of his excavation techniques was the development and utilization of a reliable method of dating, which brings us to Petrie's second major contribution. Petrie, at Tel el-Hesi, was able to refine the basic principles of pottery chronology. He realized that pottery forms were relatively standardized across certain periods within particular cultures. He also realized that changes to these forms occurred in a relatively consistent manner. Therefore, once he was able to identify the general sequence of change in the pottery forms observed throughout a site and date that sequence of change, he could date the occupational layers.[19]

Admittedly, this is an oversimplification of the actual process. Excavations of any tel and establishing a relative chronology at that site by the pottery assemblage are incredibly nuanced and difficult. However, it is not a stretch to say that Sir Flinders Petrie ushered in the era of systematic archaeology within Syria-Palestine. What's more, after Petrie's publications, the number of archaeologists coming to the region boomed. Excavations commenced at important biblical sites such as Jericho, Gezer, Meggido, Samaria, and others. The net result was that the first half of the twentieth century came to constitute the formative era of archaeology within Syria-Palestine.

Yet this is not to suggest that Petrie's principles produced an era of methodological precision. Rather, excavation efforts at the turn of and beginning of the twentieth century were enough to make any contemporary archaeologist squirm. In fact, many archaeologists today lament that they must invoke any archaeological report that antedates 1950 with extreme caution. The methodological precision of today is the product of a paradigm shift that began in the middle of the twentieth century.

By the middle of the twentieth century, a movement that had William F. Albright and his students, as well as a few others, at the center had taken

---

19. Rachel Hallote clarifies that Petrie's realization owed much to his previous work in Egypt. However, his work at Tel el-Hesi allowed the critical realization in ceramic seriation, or pottery sequencing. Rachel Hallote, " 'Bible Lands Archaeology' and 'Biblical Archaeology' in the Nineteenth and Early Twentieth Centuries," in *The Old Testament in Archaeology and History* (eds. Jennie Ebling, et. al.; Waco: Baylor University Press, 2017), 133.

hold. One of the quintessential characteristics of the movement was an expressed concern for establishing a synthesis between archaeological data and the biblical text. Albright and others explicitly discussed how archaeology could illuminate the biblical text, and their syntheses often viewed the Bible's testimony very positively. This era is often referred to as the era of "Biblical Archaeology." For example, Albright and his students synthesized the Bible's testimony in Joshua with the archaeological data of the sites mentioned in that book and ultimately articulated what is called the Conquest Model for Israel's settlement. This model essentially states that Israel's settlement of Canaan was the result of a singular lightning-fast military maneuver by the Israelites. Also during this general era, Yigael Yadin associated the building expansions of Hazor, Meggido, and Gezer with 1 Kgs 9:15. Characterized concisely, "This period in biblical archaeology is considered the heyday, when it appeared that archaeological research was continuously supporting the accounts of the biblical text."[20] However, "This initial euphoria regarding the verification of the biblical text as an accurate historical document was short-lived as the archaeological record grew."[21] Thus, the heyday of "Biblical Archaeology" was profound, but a flash in the pan.

Archaeologists during this period had come to prefer the large-scale exposure of the tel. Called the architectural approach, or the Reisner-Fisher Method, adherents to this method choose to expose large horizontal swaths and excavate massive structures at the expense of digging vertically in smaller, more controlled locations.[22] However, Dame Katheleen Kenyon ushered in a new method when she excavated Jericho in the 1950s. Instead of large-scale exposure, her excavation proceeded with smaller squares (appr. 5 x 5 feet) where the balk walls were left largely erect. Employing what would come to be known as the Kenyon-Wheeler Method, she and her team could observe the debris in various sections to contextualize finds more accurately. Yet, old habits die hard. While many archaeologists saw

20. Steven Ortiz, "Archaeology, Syro-Palestinian" in *Dictionary of the Old Testament Historical Books* (eds. Bill Arnold and Hugh Williamson; Downers Grove, IL: InterVarsity Press, 2005), 62.

21. Ortiz, "Archaeology," 62.

22. Reisner and Fisher honed their method while excavating Samaria around the turn of the century. In addition to the development of the architectural approach, they also developed classification systems for various debris, developed method of observing and analyzing intrusions into a tel's stratigraphy (such as pits and cisterns), and developed more precise method of documentation.

the benefits of a more controlled excavation, many prominent archaeologists clung to traditional methods.[23]

Along with her methodological revolution, Kenyon also came to challenge some traditional conclusions. In her most famous example, Kenyon's excavations at Jericho fundamentally undermined central tenets of the Conquest Model. Kenyon argued that the walls often assumed to be the those of the city that Joshua overran were actually Bronze Age walls and thus not datable to Joshua's period of existence. Naturally, her conclusions fueled criticisms of Albright, his students, and other conservative excavators—namely that a commitment to the Bible's testimony clouded a proper interpretation of the archaeological data. Of course, there were responses in defense of Albright and his students, but one must concede that the methodological criticisms leveled were not only well-founded but have also won the day. In fact, Albright would later step back from his initial articulation of the Conquest Theory.[24] Even his student John Bright also essentially conceded when he recognized the complexity of the archaeological data.[25]

Phase Three: Today's Archaeology in Syria-Palestine

Today, virtually all excavations in Israel employ some type of hybrid between the Kenyon-Wheeler and Reisner-Fisher methods. Excavators are committed to excavating relatively small squares so to allow for control over stratigraphic analysis. Yet because this commitment is not overly rigid, if certain variables arise, excavators will shift to large-scale exposure of a particular stratum. For example, the excavators are Tel Reḥov shifted to large-scale exposure of a particular Iron Age stratum upon finding evidence of a massive beehive installation. When all was done, they discovered one of the world's oldest apiaries in the Middle East.[26]

23. Currid, *Doing Archaeology*, 32–33.

24. W. F. Albright, *Archaeology and the Religion of Israel: The Ayers Lectures of the Colgate-Rochester Divinity School 1941* (Baltimore: Johns Hopkins, 1965), 95.

25. John Bright, *A History of Israel* (4h ed.; Louisville: Westminster John Knox, 2000), 129–33.

26. Amihai Mazar and Nava Panitz-Cohen, "It is the Land of Honey: Beekeeping at Tel Rehov," *NEA* 70.4 (2007): 202–19.

Today's excavations are also incredibly specialized and multidisciplinary. For example, it is commonplace to find at an excavation a pottery expert, geologist, zoologist, epigraphist, and others serving as members of the team. There is also an exerted effort to discuss tel excavations in context of their immediate geographical surroundings (vs. being discussed in isolation). Then there are salvage excavations that can be potentially fruitful, and surveys have also become indispensable tools for archaeology in Syria-Palestine.

Perhaps most importantly, however, today's archaeological digs proceed from a particular paradigm that was constructed during the 1960s, 1970s, and 1980s. Steven Ortiz describes it nicely.

> "Perhaps the most noteworthy change in terms of scholarship is the realization that just as biblical historians are attempting to reconstruct the past, archaeologists are attempting to reconstruct it using different data sets. Biblical archaeologists did not stop asking the questions of biblical scholarship, but they even more clearly defined the differences between archaeological data and textual data and the different hermeneutical methods used for each data set. Today there is a more complex and refined approach to the use of archaeological and textual data in reconstructing ancient society."[27]

27. Ortiz, "Archaeology," 63.

Ortiz describes a common goal, a historical goal, among biblical scholars and archaeologists. However, there are intentions and assumptions inherent to the biblical and archaeological disciplines that preclude any simplistic assimilation. These disciplines can and do converge, but that convergence requires an intelligent (vs. simplistic) synthesis.

This paradigm was forged as the tenets of "New Archaeology" were incorporated into archaeological endeavors within Syria-Palestine. Those tenets include the utilization of cultural evolutionary paradigms, the adoption of a multi-disciplinary posture, a holistic approach, the adoption of scientific methods, the utilization of ethnographic and material cultural studies, and a realization that archaeology may illuminate human patterns of thought and action.[28] Thus, archaeology came to be understood as an anthropological mode of research more than one that was directly associated with or dependent upon Biblical Studies. This is very different from the statements made about archaeology as a discipline in the CBN story on Tel Reḥov.[29] So, for a moment, let's examine this story so that a proper definition of archaeology, as well as an understanding of the relationship between archaeology and Biblical Studies, can be initially formulated.

CBN, Defining the Discipline, and this Project

Chris Mitchell's story opens by highlighting a particular structure at Tel Reḥov. Inside this oddly structured installation, certain material was found that when considered in light of one another, a striking conclusion was formed. There was cultic paraphernalia, an inscription reconstructed to read "Elisha," another inscription that mentions the family of Nimshi (of the family of King Jehu), and Tel Reḥov's geographic proximity to Elisha's stomping grounds. Taken together, Mitchell concludes that this house "might have been Elisha's." Stephen Pfann is also brought into this story, but he seems to be more convinced, finding the evidence "compelling." Then there is Cary Summers, whose comments are the most revealing. Summers

28. William Dever, "The Impact of 'New Archaeology' " in *Benchmarks in Time and Culture: Essays in Honor of Joseph A. Callaway* (eds. J. F. Drinkard, Jr, G. L. Mattingly, and J. M. Miller; Atlanta: Scholars Press, 1988): 341. Also see Dever's "The Impact of 'New Archaeology' on Syro-Palestinian Archaeology," *BASOR* 242 (1981): 15–29.

29. Chris Mitchell and Julie Stahl, "Have Archaeologists Found Prophet Elisha's House?" *Christian Broadcast Network*, Embedded Video File, 4:04, http://www1.cbn. com/video/have-archaeologists-found-prophet-elisha-rsquo-s-house?show=700club (accessed Jan 11, 2019).

declares that Tel Reḥov is just like any other site in that "every scoop of dirt proves the Bible one scoop at a time."

With each voice in this story, one detects the conviction that archae- ology *serves* Biblical Studies. In the case of Summers, this conviction is proclaimed most explicitly. Yet nestled in this story are the statements of Tel Reḥov's director, Amihai Mazar. In contrast to Summers, Mitchell, and Pfann, Mazar describes archaeology as a puzzle. According to Mazar, ar- chaeology seeks to study multiple sites over a lengthy period so that they can be synthesized to create a detailed picture about the material culture and by extension the culture itself. In other words, archaeology is a dis- cipline that focuses upon the material left by a particular culture so that a profile can be reconstructed. Thus, technically speaking, archaeology's relationship to Biblical Studies is secondary.

All of this raises the question. How does one define archaeology? Edwin Yamauchi defines it as the "study of remains of ancient civilization, frequently as the result of systematic excavations."[30] R. K. Harrison says, "Simply defined, archaeology is the science that recovers and studies the rel- ics of human antiquity."[31] According to James Battenfield, archaeology "aims for the discovery and evaluation of ancient material remains in order to ascertain the identity, nature, and extent of past civilizations and cultures."[32] One could go on and on listing specific definitions to dissect and critique them in light of specific nuances. Yet it is more prudent to define archaeol- ogy simply as the systematic excavation and study of material culture for the sake of understanding that culture or location. Or, to put it crudely, it's the study of "stuff" to understand a culture or location.

But what about the term "Biblical Archaeology?" The astute reader will have noted that while I have used the term periodically up to this point, I have displayed a preference for the phrase "archaeology in Syria-Palestine." The term "Biblical Archaeology" is an enigma. At one point in the history of biblical scholarship, it referred to a discipline intimately connected to Biblical Studies, but that is no longer the case. Now, "Biblical Archaeology" seems to refer to archaeology that informs one's understanding of the Bible,

30. Edwin Yamauchi, "Archaeology" in *Baker Encyclopedia of the Bible* (eds. Walter A. Elwell and Barry J. Beitzel; Grand Rapids: Baker Book House, 1988), 148

31. R. K. Harrison, "Archaeology and the Bible," in *Baker Encyclopedia of the Bible* (eds. Walter A. Elwell and Barry J. Beitzel; Grand Rapids: Baker Book House, 1988), 156

32. James Battenfield, "Archaeology" in *Old Testament Survey: The Message, Form, and Background of the Old Testament* (2d ed.; Grand Rapids: William B. Eerdmans, 1996), 641

directly or indirectly. Archaeology is not an endeavor that seeks to prove or disprove the biblical claims, nor is its sole concern issues of Biblical Studies. As William Dever has argued for decades, archaeology and Biblical Studies are two separate disciplines which, from time to time, enter into a dialogue and inform each other.[33] He calls these moment of dialogue "convergences," where two parallel lines of evidence come together.[34] Neither is defined by the other; neither necessarily serves the other. Therefore, the term "Biblical Archaeology" can be used to describe the application of archaeological data upon issues of Biblical Studies. This will be my intentions when I use the term in the pages that follow.

I have always appreciated Dever's methodological discussions the most. Recently, Dever published "A Critique of Biblical Archaeology: History and Interpretation," which coalesces critical points made elsewhere.[35] In this article, Dever concisely contextualizes the Biblical Archaeology movement among the frenzy of archaeological excavation in Syria-Palestine in the first half of the twentieth century in order to build a profile. Ultimately, Dever describes an "amateur affair" fueled by methodological imprecision, parochialism, and misguided agendas.[36]

According to Dever, what broke the back of the Biblical Archaeology movement were the methodological revisions of archaeology practiced outside Syria-Palestine, all of which forced the Biblical Archaeology movement to confront their tendencies. Archaeology shifted to a more anthropological posture, becoming more interdisciplinary and sophisticated in the process. Theory and method were emphasized, and excavations were forced to be more explicit in their agendas and methods. All of this, as I have stated, produced a separation. Archaeology no longer was understood to *serve* Biblical and Theological Studies. In the words of Dever, "an autonomous, more mature, more comprehensive branch

33. For a very informative interview where Dever candidly explains these and other issues, see Hershel Shanks, "Is this Man a Biblical Archaeologist? BAR Interviews William Dever—Part One," *BAR* 22.4 (1996): 30–39; 62–63; Hershel Shanks, "Is this Man a Biblical Archaeologist? BAR Interviews William Dever—Part Two," *BAR* 22.5 (1996): 31–37; 74–77.

34. William G. Dever, "Whom Do You Believe—the Bible or Archaeology," *BAR* 43.3 (May/June 2017): 44.

35. William G. Dever, "A Critique of Biblical Archaeology: History and Interpretation," in *The Old Testament in Archaeology and History* (eds. Jennie Ebeling, *et. al.*; Waco: Baylor University Press, 2017): 141–57.

36. Dever, "A Critique of Biblical Archaeology," 147.

of archaeology" took hold.[37] By implication, the quotes by Summers and others just mentioned appear to harken back to a bygone era fraught with methodological problems.

Obviously though, the separation between Biblical Studies and archaeology is not absolute. In fact, as discussed by Dever, "integrating the two disciplines" is the crux of the matter.[38] How does one responsibly fuse the results of archaeology and Biblical Studies in a way that honors the irony of things: their independence from each other and close association? Dever suggests starting independently. Meaning, biblical scholars should let archaeologists do their job! From there, after the data from both sources have been evaluated on their own terms, the goal is to identify naturally occurring intersections. Dever calls these intersections "convergences," and, according to him, "It is in the dialogue *between* two independent disciplines that our best hope for genuine new knowledge lies."[39]

But what does a dialogue between Biblical Studies and archaeology look like? Admittedly, any answer is difficult to articulate. As an example, Dever points to what is known about the Late Bronze Age/Iron Age transition as evidence for how archaeology should frame the conversations about the exodus, settlement, and Israelite origins. In the end, "Archaeology has not confirmed the biblical account as expected, to the contrary."[40] In another example, Dever points to how archaeological data has illuminated, and in a sense verified, the prophetic criticisms of the eighth century. "The abuses of which the prophets complained were real and so was their world."[41] Then there is the conversation about the development of monotheism. What do the copious Asherah Pillar Figurines, the inscriptions of Kuntillet Ajrud and Khirbet el-Qom, the Ketef Hinnom amulets, and others tells us about how monotheism developed throughout Israel's history?

In each case, it's apparent that the archaeological data enjoys a point of "contact" with the content of the Old Testament. Yet Dever's discussion creates the impression that archaeology should *drive* the conversation. This is to be expected since he believes that "after two thousand years of interpretation and reinterpretation, [the biblical texts] have yielded all

37. Dever, "A Critique of Biblical Archaeology," 149.
38. Dever, "A Critique of Biblical Archaeology," 149.
39. Dever, "A Critique of Biblical Archaeology," 152.
40. Dever, "A Critique of Biblical Archaeology," 153.
41. Dever, "A Critique of Biblical Archaeology," 154.

the information they contain."[42] Such a conviction, nevertheless, can be criticized. Dever oversimplifies things when he suggests that the biblical texts are a dry well. Consequently, a more prudent way forward must be more sophisticated.

Nevertheless, Dever is correct that the way forward exists in the so-called convergences, places where the archaeological data and the biblical text naturally connect. Connections cannot be forced, and the intentions of archaeology as a discipline must be allowed to formulate its conclusions. From there, the archaeological conclusions should collaborate with the semantic demands of the text. Neither should dictate or encroach upon the other as the delicate and respectful relationship that honors each counterpart's goals and methods *must* be preserved. Indeed, articulating what a quality dialogue will look like is difficult, but it is my hope that this work will shed some light on the conversation.

This project aims to celebrate the perpetual relationship between archaeology and Biblical Studies by discussing some of the most important archaeological finds for Old Testament Studies in order to further consider what these convergences look like. And to do this, the following chapters will exhibit a simple organization. On the one hand, what I have called broad convergences are discussed. Such convergences show how archaeological data illuminates the larger cultural realities of the Old Testament. Broad convergences may center on an element of the ancient Near Eastern thought world, institutions, or perhaps widely held literary conventions. Conversely, narrow convergences offer examples of how archaeological data explicitly informs something mentioned in the text. Examples could include a person, place, or idea.

Within each chapter, I will begin by giving a story behind each find. In addition, influential ideas about the find will be discussed in order to articulate the find's importance for Old Testament Studies. As for the selection of the finds that populate this project, they all manifest the following qualities. First, they all have produced some type of ripple effect. They have all "moved the needle," as they say. Yet their appeal has not only been to a small group of specialists. Consequently, and secondly, each of these finds have all fostered wide spread interest, among biblical scholars and non-scholars. Third, which is perhaps the most important hallmark of this project, each of these finds share a profound impact upon shaping the paradigms for Old Testament Studies and understanding the content of

42. Dever, "A Critique of Biblical Archaeology," 155.

nature of God's revelation through Scripture. By explaining how these finds continue to shape paradigms and illuminate the nature of God's revelation, discussions will distance themselves from the methodological errors of the past but honor the necessary relationship between archaeology and Biblical Studies—two separate fields that can dialogue with one another.

The finds discussed in this volume are: Mari, the Gilgamesh Epic, the Tel Dan Stele, the Taylor Prism, the pithoi found at Kuntillet Ajrud, the silver scrolls of Ketef Hinnom, Mt. Ebal, the Dead Sea Scrolls, and Ugarit.

My interest in archaeology took off during my graduate studies at Asbury Theological Seminary when I had the privilege of digging as a volunteer at Tel Reḥov, which was under the direction of Amihai Mazar at the time. As odd as it sounds, spending hours in the scorching sun excited me. Since then, I have always tried to stay current on popular topics as well as important research. As a trained biblical scholar, I think this is important. However, over recent years I have been struck by the absence of any volume that combined a discussion of several of the most important finds in an accessible way but also with an overt consideration of the proper relationship between archaeology of the Old Testament. The discussions to date, in my assessment, are either too technical, too superficial, or not methodologically sophisticated enough. Consequently, this work attempts to fill this perceived void. I want to offer an intelligent discussion (not necessarily a definitive discussion) of important finds in a way that is methodologically sensitive and informative. Time will tell if I have succeeded.

Broad Convergences

2

Mari

When I ask students about the purpose of archaeology, I count on receiving a few answers in one form or another.

"To prove that the Bible is true!"

"To find something really valuable!"

I can't say that I am surprised by such answers, particularly since most introductions to archaeology happen via *Indiana Jones*, *National Treasure*, or some other cinematic creation. Regardless whence those ideas come, all of them sensationalize the discipline. Therefore, I can't help but chuckle a bit when I see shades of disappointment creep across their faces as I jokingly explain that biblical archaeology is really days upon days of monotony in the scorching hot sun occasionally punctuated by a significant find. Worse yet, the payoff normally does not come until years after excavation has finished when archaeologists hole up in their offices in order to publish their findings.

With archaeology, there is *a lot* of meticulous digging, photographing, cataloging, starring at dirt, discussing dirt, and getting excited about dirt. However, if one is committed to the end goal, if one is in it for the long-haul and is willing to spend tremendous amounts of time synthesizing truckloads of data, then one could revolutionize the way the world understands a particular culture. *That* is the exciting part!

Tucked inside the southeast Syrian border, nestled against the border of Iraq, is Tel Hariri—the ancient site of Mari. Its excavation history started in 1933, and it exemplifies how long-term commitment can revolutionize the way a culture and cultural institutions are understood.

The Story of Mari[1]

In 1933, a French military officer[2] encountered a group of bedouin who were digging into Tel Hariri. They were burying one of their dead, and in the process, uncovered a statue. Although fragmentary, the French officer immediately knew it possessed significant value. He quickly corresponded with the Louvre in Paris, which in turn quickly dispatched André Parrot to begin systematic excavations at the site. The logistical hurdles were navigated very quickly, for within a matter of months the French had cleared the necessary paperwork and were on the ground excavating the site.

Tel Hariri has undergone systematic excavation relatively continuously since 1933 by three different directors.[3] André Parrot lead excavations from the dig's inception through 1978. In 1979, Jean-Claude Margueron assumed control, and he handed the reigns to Pascal Butterlin in 2005. Although, there has been the occasional pause in excavations due to international crises. The seventh season was delayed due to World War II, and the Suez Crisis delayed the eleventh season. Currently, the aftermath of ISIS's control of Syria and the Syrian civil war prevents any further work.

Situated approximately two kilometers from the bank of the Euphrates River, Tel Hariri lays in a valley that connects major trade routes in Syria with the Mesopotamia plains. Thus, "Mari appears as a city ideally situated to control the traffic which travels down the river as well as over land between these two poles."[4] Even more impressive, there is evidence of a series of canals that linked the ancient city with the main body of the Euphrates

1. The summary offered here has leaned heavily on the following: Stephanie Dalley, *Mari and Karana: Two Old Babylonian Cities* (2d ed.; Piscataway, NJ: Gorgias Press, 2002); Wolfgang Heimpel, *Letters to the King of Mari: A New Translation, with Historical Introduction, Notes, and Commentary* (Mesopotamian Civilizations; Winona Lake, IN: Eisenbrauns, 2003); Elizabeth Knott, A Review of Jean-Claude Margueron, *Mari, Capital of Northern Mesopotamia in the Third Millennium: The archaeology of Tell Hariri on the Euphrates*, NEA 79.1 (2016): 36–42; Amélie Kuhrt, *The Ancient Near East: c. 3000–330 BC* (Routledge History of the Ancient World; New York: Routledge, 1995) 1:95–117; Jean-Claude Margueron, *Mari, Capital of Northern Mesopotamia in the Third Millennium: The archaeology of Tell Hariri on the Euphrates* (Oxford: Oxbow Books, 2014); idem, "Mari (Archaeology)," *ABD*, 4:525–29; Wayne T. Pitard, "Before Israel: Syria-Palestine in the Bronze Ages" in *The Oxford History of the Biblical World* (ed. Michael D. Coogan; Oxford: Oxford University Press, 1998), 34–40.

2. During this time, the French were in control of Syria and Lebanon due to political negotiations after WWI.

3. Knott, A Review of *Margueron*, 37.

4. Margueron, "Mari (Archaeology)," 4:525.

River.[5] Thus, it is likely that Mari was envisioned to be and constructed as a site with the purpose of controlling traffic and accommodating trade through the region.[6]

Tel Hariri's history of occupation dates to the beginning of the third millennium BCE, and the excavators have organized its history by means of three cities. City I is the oldest layer of occupation, and Cities II and III represent the two major phases of subsequent occupation. Each phase concludes with either the abandonment or destruction of the city.[7] Mari was a circular walled city and appears to have been the capital of a kingdom comprised of four identifiable districts.[8]

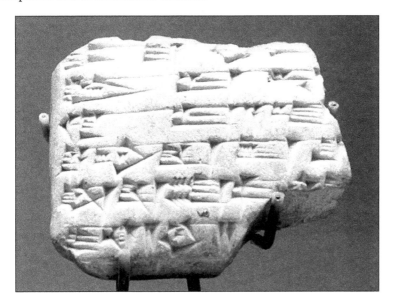

While the exact profile of City I remains enigmatic, there is evidence that Mari was a formidable urban center from the start, not the product

5. Margueron argues that the canal split the ancient site, which evidenced most clearly by the absence of approximately half the tell due to the erosion of the river up to the boundaries of the canal. Margueron, *Mari, Capital of Northern Mesopotamia*, 15–21; Margueron, "Mari (Archaeology)," 4:525. Also, see Heimpel, *Letters to the King*, 4.

6. This is further substantiated by the hostile climatological features that make agriculture essentially impossible. Margueron, *Mari, Capital of Northern Mesopotamia*, 8–9.

7. Thus, Mari was an Early Broze Age city, and the Early Bronze Age was characterized by the emergence of large urban centers. Amihai Mazar, *Archaeology of the Land of the Bible: 10000–586 BCE* (The Anchor Bible Reference Library; New York: Doubleday, 1990), 107–08. In terms of Mesopotamian chronology, Mari was an Early Dynastic city.

8. See the discussion of Heimpel, *Letters to the King*, 8–9.

of a developing village.[9] City II is arguably the best documented of all the phases, and it appears in the middle of the third millennium after a short period of abandonment. During this phase, the city appears to have undergone dramatic development and expansion. Administrative centers were constructed and/or expanded, several temple complexes appear, and the city itself seems to be have reached a level of sophistication hardly rivaled in the ancient Near East. Yet perhaps the greatest symbol of Mari's importance was its palace complex, centrally located in the city. This massive complex boasted hundreds of rooms, central courtyards, sacred enclosures, and a multi-leveled palace. Thus, "[City II] seems to have marked one of the great moments in Mari's history."[10] City II was overrun by either Sargon or Naram-Sin of the Old Akkadian Empire.

The most famous city of Tel Hariri is City III, thanks to the hoard of cuneiform texts that were unearthed beginning in the second year of excavations. City III represents Mari's final phase of occupation, and, during this phase, Mari is first ruled by a somewhat mysterious Semitic group referred to as the *Shakkanakku*. Under their leadership, City III again underwent significant reconstruction and development, evidenced in the remains of the central palace complex, temples, and administrative buildings throughout the city. However, these Semites eventually gave way to Mari's most famous ruling family—the Amorite Lim dynasty.[11] According to the literary evidence, however, the Lim dynasty's control was tumultuous, characterized by the ebbs of flows of dynastic succession, political alliances, and the influence of the Old Babylonian and Assyrian empires. For instance, Mari appears to have started out as an independent polity under Amorite control, which gave way to Assyrian control and then back to independence.[12] Also, the final king of Mari, Zimri-Lim, who appears to have been a complex personality in light of incredible internal and external pressures,[13] found

---

9. Margueron, *Mari, Capital of Northern Mesopotamia*, 25.

10. Margueron, "Mari (Archaeology)," 4:527.

11. On the Amorite phenomenon and its application to Old Testament studies, see below. For a useful summary of the difficulties in understanding and defining the Amorites, see Daniel E. Fleming, "The Amorites" in *The World Around the Old Testament: The People and Places of the Ancient Near East* (eds. Bill T. Arnold and Brent Strawn; Grand Rapids: Baker Academic, 2016), 1–30.

12. For this useful three-fold breakdown, see Pitard, "Before Israel," 35–36.

13. On the complexities of this man, including his personal history and the reconstruction of his life, see Jack M. Sasson, "The King and I: A Mari King in Changing Perceptions," *JAOS* 118 (1998): 453–70.

himself in exile when a rival seized the throne of Mari.[14] In time, with the support of other powers centered in various regions of modern day Syria, Zimri-Lim moved on Mari and regained control.

Mari was eventually destroyed by Hammurabi during the consolidation of his power and the solidification of his Old Babylonian empire. What began with a relatively simple campaign east of the Tigris transformed in a lightening quick takeover of the southern Mesopotamia region. With that base established, Hammurabi then pushed north, and in approximately 1760 BCE he violently destroyed Mari. Ironically, this violent destruction preserved the libraries, artwork, and other elements of Mari's material culture that would become so critical in reconstructing the site's history and culture of this site.

Overall, it is difficult to overstate the importance of Mari. From an architectural perspective, the city displays a level of urban planning and monumental construction rivaled by only a few. I have already mentioned of the elaborate central palace complex, an installation of hundreds of rooms that operated throughout much of Mari's existence, and in light of the content and volume of all the documents excavated there, the palace complex (vs. the temples or any other precinct) appears to have been the focal point of Mari's society, during the years assumed by the documents.

14. On Zimri-Lim's exile, see Heimpel, *Letters to the King*, 42.

With respect to the Mari's texts, excavations have uncovered over 25,000 cuneiform tablets, and a clear majority of them are dated to the final decades of Mari's existence.[15] Therefore, the final years of Mari's existence constitutes one of the most vividly documented cross-sections of ancient Near Eastern history. Thus, the words of Jean-Marie Durand are very appropriate, "The interest of the Mari texts also lies in that they provide us with a host of details on the extremely diverse and complex areas of everyday life. We actually see people pray, do business, fight, and plot, either succeeding or perishing. Few human aspects escape us."[16] Certain texts document the foods used by the court, including the so-called "King's Meal."[17] There are also audit texts, texts articulating the dynamics of the royal harem, material receipts for day to day operation, and other political realities including diplomatic and treaty correspondence. In addition, ritualistic and omen texts were found in what appear to be sacred rooms attached to the palace complex, and a smaller number of general correspondences have been excavated.[18]

There are a number of academic series devoted to the research of Mari.[19]

- *Archives royales de Mari* and *Archives royales de Mari transcrite et traduite*: The main publication series for research centering on the Mari archives. These volumes are comprised of texts in the original language, as well as transcriptions and French translations.

- *Textes cuneiforms du Lourve*: The original medium of publication for the Mari archives. It was later phased out.

- *Textes cunéiformes de Mari*: Another phased out series for the publication of the Mari archives.

---

15. Durand notes a few of the more prominent texts that fall outside the purview of the final decades. For a summary that is still useful, see, Jean-Marie Durand, "Mari, (Texts)," *ABD*, 4:529–36.

16. Durand, "Mari (Texts)," 4:536.

17. Durand, "Mari (Texts)," 4:529. A general comparison could be made with 1 Kgs 4:22–23(5:2–3) and 5:11(25), both of which list the daily consumption of Solomon's court and Hiram's court by way of Solomon's provision.

18. Oddly, any correspondence between Hammurabi and Mari during the eighteenth century has yet to be discovered. Given the cordial relationship between the two polities, at least until Hammurabi set his eyes on Mari for conquest, it is somewhat peculiar that no record has been found.

19. Also, see, Brian E. Keck, "Mari (Bibliography)," *ABD*, 4:536–38.

- *Mari, annals de recherches interdisciplinaries*: Published in Paris by Éditions recherche sur les civilisations, this publication is exclusively concerned with the research of Mari.

In addition, other prominent voices include Jack M. Sasson, who recently published a massive opus devoted to approximately seven hundred letters from the final years of Mari.[20] Similarly, Wolfgang Heimpel has collected a corpus of texts from the archive to understand the final details of Zimri-Lim's reign.[21] In a dated, but still influential study, Maurice Birot produced a 4-part study on the economy of Mari,[22] and Daniel Fleming, in his work *Democracy's Ancient Ancestors*, has reconstructed the political decision making process at Mari, shedding light on the dimorphism of Mari society in the process.[23] Yet when it comes to the intersection of Mari with issues of Biblical Studies, Abraham Malamat rises above the rest. Across three decades, Malamat studied Mari extensively with the intent of understanding how it illuminates the culture and thought-world of the Old Testament. Some of his most important work has been compiled in *Mari and the Bible*.[24]

The Implications of Mari

When it comes to the implications of Mari for understanding the Old Testament, three issues rise above the rest: the Amorites, dimorphic societies, and the dynamics of the prophetic institution. The first and second issues are roughly related and will be discussed first.

20. Jack M. Sasson, *From the Mari Archives: An Anthology of Old Babylonian Letters* (Winona Lake, IN: Eisenbrauns, 2015).

21. See note 1 above.

22. Maurice Birot, "Trois textes économiques de Mari (I)," *RA* 47 (1953): 121–30; idem, "Textes économiques de Mari (II)," *RA* 47 (1953): 161–74; idem, "Textes économiques de Mari (III)," *RA* 49 (1955): 15–31; idem, "Textes économiques de Mari (IV)," *RA* 50 (1956): 57–72.

23. Daniel Fleming, *Democracy's Ancient Ancestors: Mari and Early Collective Government* (Cambridge: Cambridge University Press, 2004).

24. Abraham Malamat, *Mari and the Bible* (VTSuppl 12; Leiden: Brill, 1998). This is a series of previously published articles on a variety of topics. Also, see *Mari and the Early Israelite Experience* (The Schweich Lectures of 1984; Oxford: Oxford University Press, 1989).

The Legacy of the Amorites and Dimorphic Societies

The testimony of Mari is an important voice for understanding the Amorite phenomenon, which refers to a broadly defined historical reality during the second and third millennia BCE. The Amorites were a diverse group of people loosely unified by a particular way of life and language. While distinguishable, the Amorites are still very enigmatic and any attempt to characterize them remains tentative. Nevertheless, they appear to be in the middle of large-scale social changes experienced across the ancient Near East that intensified during the Middle Bronze Age.[25]

The Amorites, which literally means "western" or "westerner," are referenced in a few Sumerian texts that date as far back as the third millennium BCE (MARTU). There, they are viewed negatively as outsiders, perceived to be a threat to the status quo. In fact, the disdain was so intense that an "Amorite wall" was constructed to fend off any advance into the Sumerian heartland.[26] However, any understanding of the Amorites "cannot be universalized" across history.[27] In the Sumerian texts the Amorites were a broadly defined group of people loosely connected by a mobile

25. Around the end of the third millennium BCE, the ancient Near East experienced a dramatic collapse of urban civilization. Sites that were once bustling urban centers were mysteriously abandoned. Furthermore, the archaeological record suggests that the ancient Near East entered something of a lull, or intermediate period. that lasted a few hundred years. Associated with this collapse was the collapse of the Sumerian culture, which was centered in southern Mesopotamia, and it was the Sumerians that who famously referred to building an "Amorite Wall" (see below). So, because the Amorites were villainized by a culture that would cease to exist in the wake of the collapse, and because the Amorites are documented to have been spread out across the Fertile Crescent during this period, many scholars jumped to the conclusion that the Amorites were at the center of the collapse, and possibly the impetus for it. W. F. Albright applied this general theory to the Patriarchs, specifically Abraham. He suggested that he was a part of the Amorite migrations, a theory which became known as the Amorite Hypothesis. Today, Albright's Amorite Hypothesis, classically articulated, no longer holds water. Moreover, the collapse of the Early Bronze urban culture is likely the result of a multi-faceted process of events rather than a singular culture. As for the marked changes in the archaeological record, many today understand it more to be indicative of a pronounced shift in day-to-day life than the incursion of outside cultures. What remains consistent throughout the history of research is the presence of the Amorites throughout the region during the transition between the third and second millennia BCE. The details of their influence will continue to be dated for some time.

26. Fleming, "The Amorites," 5.

27. Fleming, "The Amorites," 8.

pastoralist way of life and the perception that they were outsiders.[28] Yet the Sumerian evidence only articulates an early southern Mesopotamia perspective. In the Mari archives, dated hundreds of years after the Sumerian texts, the Amorites were an identifiable polity and culture that was geographically diverse but loosely associated by language. Furthermore, it appears to have been something of a relative term, sometimes pitted against the "Akkadian."[29] Interestingly, Fleming has argued that the common term for Amorite, *amurrû*, appears to be fading from usage in the Mari archives when making a general reference to mobile pastoralism.[30] Despite these difficulties, it's clear that the Mari archives still present a critical cross-section for understanding the Amorite phenomenon.

This Mesopotamian testimony is important because these realities are loosely echoed in the Old Testament's testimony. The Amorites appear in the Old Testament via the term אֱמֹרִי. Interestingly, of the eighty-seven occurrences, seventy-one of them appear between Genesis and Judges. Therefore, as noted by Fleming, the Amorites are remembered predominately as a pre-monarchal polity, which roughly reflects the extra-biblical testimony of a Bronze Age reality.[31] In addition, the Old Testament remembers a loosely defined but distinguishable polity spread throughout the region (e.g. Gen 15:21; Ex 3:17; 13:5; Deut 7:1). More specifically, the Amorites occupied the Promised Land prior to Israel's settlement, as well as parts of the Trans-Jordan regions. Overwhelmingly associated with the hill country (e.g. Josh 10:6; 11:3), which was traditionally associated with a pastoral way of life, the Old Testament also occasionally distinguishes them from the Canaanites on the plains (e.g. Josh 5:1). Yet most importantly, the Amorites are remembered negatively, as outsiders that needed to be purged due to their religious non-conformity to the Yahwistic ideal. Despite this, the Old Testament testifies that the Amorites remained among Israel well into the monarchal period, even being called out as an entity within Solomon's conscripted labor force (1 Kgs 9:20).

When it comes to understanding dimorphism and its implications for the social makeup of ancient Near East during the Middle Bronze Age, one must begin by understanding that it refers to the presence of identifiable and separate elements within a society that collaborate for the integrity of said

28. Fleming, "The Amorites," 5–7.

29. Fleming, "The Amorites," 8–15.

30. Fleming, "The Amorites," 13.

31. Fleming, "The Amorites," 15–17.

society. In the case of Mari, its documents reveal a daily interaction between sedentary and pastoral elements, whether in the case of disseminating natural resources, producing a particular product, or resolving disagreements. In fact, each element was integral to the integrity of Zimri-Lim's kingdom. As stated by Fleming, with Zimri-Lim "we confront the undeniable integration of tribal identity into a large city-based kingdom so that tribes, on the one hand, and their mobile pastoralist herdsman, on the other, cannot be relegated to the periphery of ancient Mesopotamian politics or society."[32] Such dimorphism can explain elements of the Patriarchal traditions. For example, Abraham "pitched his tent" between two established settlements (Gen 12:6; 13:3; NRSV), Bethel and Ai, and Lot "settled among the cities of the Plain and moved his tent as far as Sodom" (Gen 13:12; NRSV). More negatively, the herders of Isaac quarreled with rival herders over watering rights, an issue that appears to have been precipitated by the fact that the local sedentary population had stopped the wells up after the death of Abraham (Gen 26:17–30). Also, when Jacob finally settled in the vicinity of Shechem, he purchased a plot of land (Gen 33:18–20). Indeed, more examples could be pointed out, but these examples suffice to demonstrate how the Patriarchal narrative coincide with the general cultural milieu. However, as we shall see, when it comes to "proving" the historicity of the Patriarchal narratives, things are much more complicated.

The Dynamics of the Prophetic Institution

Mari has proven to be an invaluable resource for understanding the dynamics of biblical prophecy. Leaning heavily on approximately fifty-five texts from the Mari archives,[33] scholars have been able to construct a useful profile of the prophetic office, which goes a long way in explaining the dynamics of the biblical phenomenon.

The Old Testament uses several terms to designate a prophet. First, there is *nābî'* (נָבִיא), which is widely attested across the Old Testament and essentially functions as the office's *terminus technicus*.[34] Yet there is also

32. Fleming, *Democracy's Ancient Ancestors*, 231.

33. Abraham Malamat, "Intuitive Prophecy – A General Survey" in *Mari and the Bible* (VTSuppl 12; Leiden: Brill, 1998), 60.

34. For example, "The term *nābî'* came to have a very inclusive range of meaning, serving as a catchall designation for all kinds of religious types [of prophets]." Joseph Blenkinsopp, *A History of Prophecy in Israel* (rev. enl.; Louisville: Westminster John

"man or woman of God" (' *iš* ' *ᵉlōhīm*; ' *ešet* ' *ᵉlōhīm*; אֲשֶׁת אֱלֹהִים;אִישׁ אֱלֹהִים),
"seer" (*rō' eh*; רֹאֶה), "visionary" (*hōzeh*; חֹזֶה), and others. So, while there may
be a preferred term, the Old Testament suggests that the prophetic office

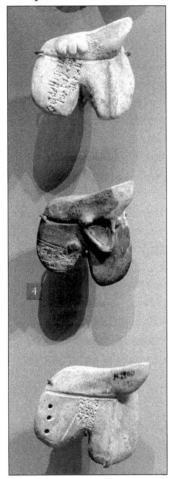

cannot be reduced to any single term. Similarly, there are several terms throughout the
Mari archives for the prophetic institution.
There is the term *nabûm*, which is linguistically related to *nābī'*,[35] but occurs only
sparingly.[36] In addition, there is the use of
assinnum, qammātum, āpilum, and even
sangûm.[37] Most commonly, however,
muhhum appears, and this refer to professional prophets that often exhibited an ecstatic or frenetic method of prophecy.[38]

It's unclear to what extent the names
allude to the specific type of prophetic
action. For example, the biblical term
"seer" has been linked to the notion that
the prophet "saw" the message to be communicated. This is possible, but one must
concede that over time the titles became
more indicative of the office rather than
any method of action.[39] When it comes to
the method and actions of the prophetic
office, Mari offers an intriguing parallel to
what is attested to in the Old Testament.
On the one hand, Mari speaks to the standard methods of prophetic action, such as
magic, omens, oracles, and extispicies.

Knox, 1996), 28.

35. *HALOT*, 2:661–62.

36. Malamat, "Intuitive Prophecy," 66.

37. The *sangûm* refers to a priest, which according to at least one text was endowed
with a prophetic dream. Malamat, "Intuitive Prophecy," 66.

38. Malamat, "Intuitive Prophecy," 66.

39. Assuming a title is indicative of the type of action is an example of an etymologi-
cal fallacy, which assumes that the historical origins of a word always dictate meaning.

For example, Mari text ARM 26 206 recounts an omen delivered to King Zimri Lim whereby a prophet eats a part of a lamb to symbolize the "devouring that will take place" if some taboo material is not returned.[40] To be clear, such actions are also a part of the Old Testament tradition. For example, Jeremiah buries a cloth (Jer 13) and Ezekiel eats food cooked over human excrement (Ezek 4).

On the other hand, Mari attests to non-inductive methods of prophecy, also called intuitive prophecy. Intuitive prophets were those who may or may not have been "professional prophets"[41] and performed their duties by a variety of methods not rooted in the observation of concrete phenomena.[42] Hays describes such prophets as "direct mouthpieces."[43] First, prophets spontaneously uttered their messages as a result of experiencing some type of divine "inspiration." This is similar to what one reads throughout the Old Testament, as when the "word of the Lord" would come to the prophets. Second, prophetic messages at Mari are linked to a conscious mission or course of action. That is, the prophetic message reaches beyond mere information to serve a larger purpose, a larger message.[44] For example, one Mari text recounts a type of salvation oracle for Zimri-Lim in light of Hammurabi's maneuvers against his kingdom. In this case, the prophecy functions to encourage the king and recalibrate his focus toward future restoration, which is similar to the restoration oracles found throughout biblical prophecy. Third, Mari attests to ecstatic episodes of prophecy (broadly defined).[45] Similar episodes are recounted in 1 Samuel by Saul's prophetic "episodes" (1 Sam 10:9–16; 19:18–24).

40. For a discussion, see Christopher B. Hays, *Hidden Riches: A Sourcebook for the Comparative Study of the Hebrew Bible and Ancient Near East* (Louisville: Westminster John Knox, 2014), 239–43.

41. Malamat discussed "lay prophets," which appear to have been non-professional prophets based on their juxtaposition and discussion opposite of prophets officially associated with some central power structure, such as a court or temple. Malamat, "Intuitive Prophecy," 72.

42. For these definitions, see Hays, *Hidden Riches*, 236.

43. Hays cites the work of Martti Nissinen. See Hays, *Hidden Riches*, 236.

44. Abraham Malamat, "Prophetic Revelations in Mari and the Bible," in *Mari and the Bible* (VTSuppl 12; Leiden: Brill, 1998), 90–94.

45. Malamat asserts that this characteristic should remain broadly defined, allowing it to encompass anything from "autosuggestion to the divinely infused dream." When frenzy does occur, it is unclear if it was "accompanied by loss of senses." Malamat, "Intuitive Prophecy," 61.

Consequently, Mari offers a valuable parallel to many methods memorialized in the Old Testament. Yet one should be conscious not to take the comparison too far. "These particular characteristics . . . link the diviner prophet at Mari with the Israelite prophet more than any other divinatory type known in the Ancient Near East."[46] However, "[T]he analogy between prophecy at Mari and that is Israel is still presently vague, the two being set apart by a gap or more than six centuries. Furthermore, many of the intervening links are 'missing.' It would thus be premature to regard Mari as a prototype of prophecy in Israel."[47]

Also related to the notion of intuitive prophecy is the issue of credibility. According to one Mari text, a piece of hair and a garment accompany a message for reasons that appear to be those of authentication.[48] Elsewhere, assurances were made to Zimri-Lim that the prophetic word he was about to hear or just heard was credible.[49] Thus, Mari is similar to the Old Testament when it testifies to concerns for authenticity, a phenomenon at the heart of some of the great prophetic conflicts found in the Old Testament (e.g. Jer 28; Amos 7:10–17).

Mari also shows how prophets are distinguished by their association to the central power structures. Prophets are either central or peripheral. Central prophets have a marked association with a society's central power structures, such as the royal court or the temple, and peripheral prophets are linked to the fringes of society. Indeed, the Mari archives show that an overwhelming number of the prophesies are intended for King Zimri-Lim. But the recipient of the message is not indicative of a prophet's social location. According to Malamat, prophecy at Mari tended to be "marginal," as a majority of the prophets hailed from the fringes of the kingdom.[50] This is similar to many of the Old Testament prophets. For example, Micah came from the outskirts of the Judean territory (Moresheth), Jeremiah was from a banished priestly line from Anathoth (cf. 1 Kgs 2:26–27), and Elijah was a prophet from the fringes of Israelite territory. Yet the Old Testament also testifies to central prophets, such as Nathan and Isaiah. Nevertheless, in every case, the function of the prophet was essentially the same—to be guardians of the covenant and confront the status quo when necessary.

46. Malamat, "Intuitive Prophecy," 61.
47. Malamat, "Intuitive Prophecy," 64.
48. Malamat, "Intuitive Prophecy," 78.
49. Malamat, "Intuitive Prophecy," 79.
50. Malamat, "Intuitive Prophecy," 62.

In summary, Mari provides a valuable cross-section for understanding the prophetic office, which compliments the more lengthy and diachronic picture offered by the Old Testament. Most importantly, Mari allows one to understand how biblical prophecy was truly an ancient Near Eastern phenomenon. Prophets simultaneously served a theological and sociological function. They were intermediaries, carrying forth the divine message to the community at large. Yet prophetic credibility was not restricted by the prophet's social location. Whether a central or peripheral prophet, whether associated with the central power structures or not, the prophet enjoyed the sanction of the divine and utilized a variety of methods to bring the divine word to bear upon a situation or experience. Many of those experiences can be broadly defined as times of crisis, whether from internal or external crises.

Before this chapter concludes, it is prudent to comment on the implications Mari has for the Patriarchal Narratives. Given that Mari is an important voice for understanding the dynamics of dimorphic societies and the Amorite phenomenon, both of which are issues relevant to the narratives of Abraham, Isaac, and Jacob, what does all this data mean for assessing the historicity of the Old Testament, particularly the Patriarchal narratives?

To say that Mari speaks directly to the historicity of the Patriarchal narratives would be incorrect. Questions of historicity are incredibly nuanced, and whether it be dimorphism, the Amorite phenomenon, or the prophetic institution, the connections between Mari and the Old Testament are not overly specific. However, the inability of the Mari evidence as it is currently understood to speak to the historicity of the Old Testament or the Patriarchal Narratives in anything other than generalities does not diminish the site's importance. We could not speak of the prophetic institution in such detail without the data from Mari. Neither would we be as informed about dimorphism or the Amorites without Mari. Ultimately, the student should take what the data offers, which in this case is an awareness of general but important cultural realities. Armed with this information, the student can reconstruct a backdrop against which specific claims that speak to the Old Testament's historicity can organically and powerfully bubble to the surface.

3

The Gilgamesh Epic

The Gilgamesh Epic is one of the great narratives of ancient Mesopotamia. It recounts one man's quest to understand the fundamental realities of human existence. Yet the discovery of this ancient narrative is story in its own right. Linked to the earliest excavations in Mesopotamia, all of which were marked by a concern for riches and international prestige more than understanding Mesopotamian culture, the discovery of the Gilgamesh Epic required scholars to analyze and synthesize many individual clay tablets compiled from different locations. Ultimately, the Gilgamesh Epic provides valuable insight into some of the fundamental literary dynamics of the Old Testament, making it an invaluable comparative tool.

After a summary of the narrative's content, a sketch of the excavations of Layard, Rassam, and Smith will be offered before a discussion of the importance of the Gilgamesh Epic concludes the chapter.

The Gilgamesh Epic: A Summary[1]

The Gilgamesh Epic begins by praising the feats of Gilgamesh, a historical king of Uruk. According to the opening lines, Gilgamesh is renowned for a quest that took him to the edges of the world (I.1,3) where he saw "the foundation of the country" (I.1,4) and brought back secrets of the human existence (I.7–8). He is also praised for his building campaigns that eventually produced a famous wall surrounding Uruk (I.11), the construction of sacred storehouses (I.12), and the reconstruction of destroyed cult

---

1. The synopsis here is indebted heavily to A. R. George's translation of the Standard Babylonian version. See A. R. George, *The Babylonian Gilgamesh Epic: Introduction, Critical Edition, and Cuneiform Texts* (2 vols; Oxford: Oxford University Press, 2003), 1:531–735. All quotations of the Gilgamesh Epic come from George's work unless stated otherwise.

centers (I.43). Gilgamesh was "endowed with a superb physique," (I.29) was of "perfect strength" (I.35), and was both "perfect and terrible" (I.37). Most notably, Gilgamesh was two-thirds divine (I.48), crafted by the gods themselves (I.49ff.).

Yet Gilgamesh was not benevolent. He wielded his gifts and abilities at the expense of his subjects. Tablet I describes how Gilgamesh would let "no son go free to his father" (I.68), nor a "daughter go free to her mother" (I.72), nor a "girl go free to her bridegroom" (I.76). Gilgamesh "wrongfully vexed" the men of Uruk (I.67) and behaved with "fierce arrogance" (I.69). In time, the people of Uruk cried out because of their plight, and the gods heard them. In turn, the gods created a wild man that could rival Gilgamesh in strength and ability. Enkidu was his name. As a strong man, with matted long hair, Enkidu was, literally, a man of the wilderness. He ate grass, drank from the natural watering holes, and was at home among the beasts (I.103–12).

According to the narrative, one of Gilgamesh's subjects encounters Enkidu in the wilderness. That servant agitated that Enkidu did not allow him to perform his duties (I.129–33), complains to Gilgamesh, who then instructs him to usher a local prostitute into the wilderness to seduce Enkidu. Her seduction works, for after a lengthy period of decadence, Enkidu's purity, and thus his lordship over the beasts, vanishes (I.199–200). No longer comfortable in the wilderness, Enkidu journeys to Uruk at the urging of the prostitute to challenge Gilgamesh's authority.

The showdown between Gilgamesh and Enkidu happens in the midst of a ritualistic celebration. Enkidu blocks the entry of the place where the ritual is to commence, and an intense fight ensues. Bodies are thrown about, crashing and destroying just about everything. Yet apparently, the fight proved Enkidu's worth, for instead of driving them apart and intensifying any animosity, an intimate relationship between the two blossoms. In fact, Gilgamesh decides, after some debate (II.272–299) that he and Enkidu shall travel to the forests of Lebanon to face off against Humbaba, the guardian of the famous Cedar Forest whose "speech was fire and breath was death" (II.222).

Gilgamesh and Enkidu travel for a lengthy period and experience a series of dreams along the way. They eventually arrive at the Cedar Forest fully intact. Initially, they are smitten by the majesty of the forest but ultimately descend into its depths to find Humbaba. When they cross paths with the guardian, Humbaba welcomes them by hurling insults at them, targeting Enkidu in particular. He even asks why he has persuaded Gilgamesh to come on such a foolish quest (V.85–94). Gilgamesh, in turn, appears to be paralyzed by fear, which only engenders Enkidu's chastisement (V.99–107). Eventually, the god Shamash appears, and his cosmic efforts allow Gilgamesh and Enkidu to subdue Humbaba and gain victory.

Humbaba begs for his life, but this ultimately fails. He is beheaded, and Gilgamesh and Enkidu return to Uruk full of plunder and reveling in their well-deserved fame. Upon their return, the two are celebrated. While cleaning up from the battle, Gilgamesh is approached by the goddess Ishtar, who insists that he become her bridegroom (VI.7). Gilgamesh rebuffs her, which in turn sets her off. "Furious," she goes "weeping" before the feet of her father and accuses Gilgamesh of "heaping abuse" on her (VI.79–86). Her father questions whether this situation was in fact her doing, but he nevertheless grants Ishtar control over the cosmic Bull of Heaven, which she intends to use to terrorize Uruk. But Ishtar's plans are to no avail. Enkidu and Gilgamesh team up again to subdue and slay the beast. And if this was not enough, Enkidu mutilates the bull and throws a portion of that bull at Ishtar while she is attempting to curse Gilgamesh and Uruk (VI.151–57).

The epic then shifts to a meeting of the pantheon, which takes inventory of the duo's exploits. The gods eventually determine that Enkidu must die. Of course, Enkidu entreats the pantheon for mercy when he learns of his potential fate, and in the process, he even desires to curse the harlot who seduced and brought him from the wilderness in the first place. Unfortunately, such anger only seals his fate, and he eventually dies.

Gilgamesh then enters a period of intense morning for his beloved friend, spiraling out of control emotionally in the process. "Weeping bitterly as he roamed the wild" (IX.2), Gilgamesh ponders his eventual death but also remembers the famed Utnapishtum, the once mortal man who gained immortality. Realizing this, he endeavors to find Utnapishtum and discover the secret of eternal life.

Gilgamesh's journey brings him to the borders between the earthly and heavenly realms. On Mt. Mashu, Gilgamesh encounters a scorpion man who obliges to point him in the direct of Utnapishtum. Later, on the shores of the sea that separates the heaven and early realms, Gilgamesh encounters Shiduri, who initially bars Gilgamesh from the gate as the king's broken physique has rendered him unrecognizable. After some persuasion, Shiduri identifies Urshanabi who is the boatman that can take him to Utnapishtum. Gilgamesh then forces himself onto the boat (X.92–108) only to find that his violent incursion onto the boat destroyed the means to maneuver the boat across the ocean. At the suggestion of Urshanabi, Gilgamesh then cuts down a host of trees to fashion oars to paddle across the sea. Eventually, the boat reaches the distant shore where Utnapishtum has been watching from afar. He too does not recognize Gilgamesh because of his brokenness, but he eventually shares the story of a great flood that resulted in his immortality.

His story begins in the city of Shuruppak, "situated on the banks of the Euphrates" and a place where the gods lived among humanity (XI.12–13). For a reason not articulated, the gods decided to send a Deluge to wipe out humanity.[2] However, the god Ea secretly divulged the plan to Utnapishtum, commanding him to "demolish the house" and "build a boat" (XI.24). Utnapishtum obeyed and constructed a floating cube.[3] But in the process, Utnapishtum necessarily deceived the other members of the community, for they had become interested in his course of action. Utnapishtum informed them that he was commanded to leave Shuruppak and live with Ea. If they would only help him in his endeavor, the city would receive ample rain (XI.43). In turn, craftsmen and workers of all kinds descended upon Utnapishtum's worksite, and Utnapishtum kept them happy with food, drink, and parties.

Upon completion of this multi-leveled vessel, Utnapishtum loaded it with riches, animals, and craftsmen, presumably to perpetuate his culture and livelihood (XI.81–86). When the storms arrived, they were so violent that the gods "curled up like dogs, lying out in the open" (XI.115). The gods screamed unconsolably only to immediately regret their decision to send the Deluge (XI. 118–26). After a full six days of storms, the rain subsided and Utnapishtum finally beheld the destruction. People were turned to clay and the Mesopotamia plain looked like an ocean. At the site of this, Utnapishtum wept.

When the water level eventually subsided, the boat came to rest on Mt. Nimush. Utnapishtum waited one week before he sent out a series of three birds. First, there was a dove, but it returned. Next was the swallow, which also returned. Finally, he sent a raven, which did not come back. This, understandably, was interpreted as a sign to unload the and offer sacrifices.

---

2. In an earlier version, noise is given as the reason for the Deluge. However, the Standard Babylonian Version omits any reason.

3. "The boat that you are going to build, her dimensions shall all correspond; her breadth and her length shall be the same" (XI.28–30).

Upon smelling the aroma, the gods swarmed around it "like flies" (XI.163) and they condemned Enlil from attending as the Deluge was his plan. However, Enlil eventually showed up, and when he realized that humanity was not wiped out, he became angry. Naturally, then, an argument ensued. Yet Enlil ultimately conceded and deified Utnapishtum and his wife.[4]

In the end, Utnapishtum emphasizes to Gilgamesh that immortality is beyond his reach. Utnapishtum's situation was anomalous, unique and cannot be duplicated. By implication, Gilgamesh's quest has been futile. Moreover, to prove a point about Gilgamesh's humanity, Utnapishtum challenges him to stay awake for a week. Of course, Gilgamesh falls asleep immediately (XI. 210–11). As he sleeps, Unapishtum commands his wife to bake food to prove to Gilgamesh that he has been sleeping, for Utnapishtum anticipates Gilgamesh's denial. After a short period of denial, Gilgamesh is forced to resign himself to his humanity, and prepares to go back to Uruk with Urshanbi, who had been removed of his duties for allowing Gilgamesh access to Utnapishtum in the first place.

Yet, ironically, Utnapishtum reveals one last secret. A certain plant grows magically at the bottom of the cosmic waters, the Apshu. If Gilgamesh were somehow to obtain it, rejuvenation may be his. So, by tying heavy stones to himself, Gilgamesh descends to the bottom of those waters, retrieves the plant, and then prepares to return to Uruk. On his way back, however, Gilgamesh rests near a pool of cool water and a snake stealthily carries off the plant, consumes it, and immediately sheds its skin. When Gilgamesh realizes this, he weeps. From there, Urshanbi and Gilgamesh can only return to Uruk where they behold the majesty of the city from the top of its walls.

Tablet 12 is odd. Enkidu is alive again, and the text tells us that he decides to descend into the netherworld to retrieve a set of toys that were gifted to Gilgamesh for his service to the gods. Gilgamesh counsels Enkidu not to draw attention to himself while there, but, unfortunately, Gilgamesh's counsel proves futile as Enkidu assumes his place alongside the dead. In turn, Gilgamesh enters a period of intense mourning whereby he entreats the gods to bring Enkidu back. However, in place of resurrection, Enkidu's shade visit's Gilgamesh, who decides to interrogate Enkidu so to understand the secrets of the afterlife. According to Enkidu, dying at a ripe old age with

---

4. For example, "In the past Utnapishtum was one of mankind, but now Utnapishtum and his wife shall be like us gods" (XI.203–04).

a large family capable of performing memorial rituals is ideal, for proper memorial rites are critical to one's existence in the afterlife.

Finding the Gilgamesh Epic[5]

The Gilgamesh Epic was not found all at once. What scholars know about this massive literary epic stems from the synthesis of various fragments found across Mesopotamia, Syria, and Hattusha (the capital of the ancient Hittite empire). Moreover, how each of those fragments were discovered is a story worthy of recounting. But alas, there is not the time or space for each account. Nevertheless, the excavations of Mesopotamia in the middle of the nineteenth century enjoy prominence, for they introduced the world to Gilgamesh and the epic that bears his name.

In the initial stages of the nineteenth century, fascination with the Middle East and its treasures was increasing rapidly. Starting with Napoleon Bonaparte and his treks across Egypt, traveler gave way to traveler and excitement seemed to grow by the month. Into this atmosphere stepped Henry Rawlinson, who was credited for deciphering cuneiform, the writing system of ancient Mesopotamia. His accomplishment blew the doors off the possibilities for understanding the ancient Near East. It was into such an exciting and potentially fruitful context that Austen Henry Layard stepped.

Layard was born in France to an affluent British family. He moved across Europe only to eventually find himself back in England, taking a job with one of his kin as a legal clerk. Yet the cramped confines of urban London ultimately wore the adventurous Layard thin. As described by Fagan, "The wintery streets of London were a far cry from the open spaces of Italy. Ambitious Layard felt caged in and stultified at the prospect of steady legal career."[6] Then, at the urging of his uncle, Layard set off to open a branch of operations in Ceylon, modern day Sri Lanka. There, Layard would meet Charles Edward Mitford, a meeting that would alter Layard's future and satisfy his itch for adventure.

The two of them decided upon a lengthy period of travel across Europe and into Asia Minor. As the two trekked through the Levant, Mitford

5. This summary is heavily indebted to Brian Fagan's work, which includes countless more details. Brian D. Fagan, *Return to Babylon: Travelers, Archaeologists, and Monuments in Mesopotamia* (rev. ed.; Boulder: University Press of Colorado, 2007).

6. Fagan, *Return to Babylon*, 110.

and Layard were eventually separated. Layard continued southward on his own, only to be beaten and robbed by the locals of Petra. He nevertheless took it in stride and eventually rejoined Mitford in Aleppo. From there, they headed for modern day Mosul and eventually the southern reaches of Iraq. All of this helped establish Layard as a seasoned traveler familiar with the nuances and indigenous cultures of the Middle East. So, when Layard arrived back in Constantinople, the British ambassador was keen to keep Layard on staff. In fact, this fledgling political career proved very beneficial in his later endeavors as an archaeologist.

According to Fagan, many, including Henry Rawlinson, eventually solicited the British government to appoint Layard as leader of excavations in Mesopotamia.[7] The French were already in the region, and so it is likely that nationalistic ambitions were also fueling this push. Nevertheless, in 1845 Layard was given a short appointment to excavate the mounds outside of modern-day Mosul. Immediately, Layard's appointment paid off. Layard quickly found two palace complexes, including one that belonged to one of the final kings of the Neo-Assyrian Empire—Esarhaddon. In addition, his excavations yielded copious inscriptions and figurines. Just a few days later, Layard found inscriptions dating to Tiglath Pilesar III, who is probably the most notorious monarch of the Neo-Assyrian Empire. Methodologically, Layard's excavation techniques were incredibly crude, almost barbaric, and certainly reflected the priorities of the age.

> "He simply tunneled into huge mounds and went on digging until he hit a fine sculpture or a stone-walled palace room. His deep tunnels lead along the walls and rooms and ignored or destroyed the contents of the chambers. Although Layard was more conscientious then his contemporaries, he never forgot that he continuation of the excavations depended upon a steady flow of fine sculptures to export. Everything was subordinate to that objective."[8]

Yet during his excavations, appeasing his benefactors was not his most immediate concern. As he dug, Layard had to keep the local polities at bay. So, he honored their local customs of hospitality through periodic celebrations and systematically greasing the wheels belonging the local sheikhs. Overall though, Layard showed a "remarkable sensitivity and

---

7. Fagan, *Return to Babylon*, 114–15.
8. Fagan, *Return to Babylon*, 120.

skill in managing the human side of excavations."[9] Still, the presence of westerners digging on local land, only to export the content of that land away, created a tense dynamic.

Layard retired initially after digging only two years. In 1847, Layard packed up shop only to find himself celebrated as a celebrity across Europe. His shipments were the talk of the town, and when he arrived back in London the media outlets could not satisfy their hunger for his stories. Perhaps it was this fame that pushed Layard to secure another grant for another dig, but in the end public opinion, no matter how fierce, could not sway the British government. His request was denied.

In 1849, approval for another excavation was given. So, Layard returned to Mosul, and during his second excavation he decided for a two-pronged approach, focusing on the simultaneous excavation of two mounds. It was a good thing as well, for during his excavation of the mound called Kuyunik he unearthed the palaces of Ashurbanipal and Sennacherib. From the former, Layard's successor Rassam would find perhaps the greatest library of antiquity. From the latter, Layard would find the most beautifully violent wall decoration of antiquity—Sennacherib's golden reliefs recounting the bloody siege and destruction of Lachish in 701 BCE.

It's difficult to overstate the significance of Layard. His work intensified excitement over Mesopotamia and the Fertile Crescent. In fact, in the wake of Layard's work the British government would quickly send people farther south into the heart of ancient Babylon hoping to duplicate Layard's successes. While the finds there were not as numerous as those of Layard and northern Mesopotamia, the finds from the south were significant. They were just not be fully appreciated until decades later. The discovery of Sumer, Ur, and the palace of Nabonidus were all apart of these southern excavations. Perhaps most importantly, Layard inspired a whole generation of scholars and archaeologists after him, and one of those would be his assistant, Hormuzd Rassam, who would eventually take over his excavations at ancient Nineveh.

Rassam was similar to Layard in the sense that he understood the politics of archaeology. He knew whom to satisfy and what steps to take if someone of importance felt slighted. This quality was invaluable because by the time Rassam was on the scene the locals were beginning to realize more and more the value of their property.

9. Fagan, *Return to Babylon*, 121.

Rassam did not enjoy the immediate success of Layard. In fact, he was almost cut-off. Yet as the story goes, in a last-ditch effort, Rassam took a small group of workers to dig at night so not to catch the attention of the landowner who was in the process of shutting them down. On the third night of digging, Rassam and his men finally hit pay-dirt. They unearthed a relief that led to sculptures and then more treasure. He had found his target in the eleventh-hour, and his night digging quickly turned to day-time digging as he rushed to uncover as much as possible as quickly as possible. During this process, Rassam unearthed the main portion of Ashurbanipal's textual archives. In the end, he crated up over twenty thousand tablets to ship back to the British Museum. The contents of these crates would change the way the Old Testament was understood as ancient literature.

Because Rassam and others did not immediately understand the value of the tablets, when the crates arrived in London they were unpacked and analyzed at a comfortable pace. No one seemed to be in a hurry, and Samuel Birch eventually assumed the responsibility of studying and publishing the texts. Birch was apparently very hospitable and eager to involve young aspiring scholars. One of those scholars was George Smith, a self-educated and "classic ivory-tower scholar."[10] He astonished many by teaching himself cuneiform and bucked the established methods of translation and analysis as he valued intuition over familiarity with grammar and syntax.[11] While unorthodox in his day, his idiosyncrasies worked. Eventually, Henry Rawlinson solicited the British Museum on his behalf to secure his full-time employment.

Without a doubt George Smith is most famous for is 1872 lecture to the Society of Biblical Archaeology, where he discussed his translation and work on the "Chaldean Account of the Deluge." There, to a laser focused audience, which included Prime Minister Gladstone,[12] Smith discussed how elements of the narrative bore remarkable similarity with Genesis. He recounted how all the major themes were present in the Mesopotamian account, all the way down to the sending of birds to determine if the flood waters abated. Moreover, Smith projected how it was likely that there would be other accounts of the same narrative elsewhere, only waiting to be found. Naturally, the following uproar was not unexpected. What was unexpected was that the

10. Fagan, *Return to Babylon*, 189.

11. Paul Kriwaczek, *Babylon: Mesopotamia and the Birth of Civilization* (New York: Thomas Dunne Books, 2010), 67.

12. Kriwaczek, *Babylon*, 68.

Daily Telegraph, and not the British Museum, funded the expedition back to Mosul, charging Smith to search for more tablets.

Many scholars admit that Smith was a questionable choice to lead the excavation. He was a brilliant academic and a linguist, but he lacked the sensitivity and intuition regarding the human dynamics of an excavation, qualities that proved to be beneficial on a number of occasions for his predecessors. So, he struggled with the politics on the ground, not to mention the intricacies of digging. However, what Smith lacked in interpersonal skills and methodological rigor he made up with intellect. He was essentially fluent in Akkadian, which meant that he could evaluate the worth of any inscription on the spot. So, it seems that what characterized him as a scholar also characterized him as an archaeologist—an awkward and unorthodox scholar who was uniquely effective.

In 1873, Smith dispatched word to the Daily Telegraph that he found more inscriptions to fill in the gaps of the Deluge Account. In turn, the newspaper rewarded his efforts by ordering him to return to England. However, the British Museum was not finished with him. As soon as he returned to London, preparations were made to send him back to Mosul. On his return trip, he did not disappoint. By the end of 1874, Smith was employing approximately 600 diggers and excavating over three thousand tablets. However, the local governmental polities made everything difficult. They constantly harassed him and even accused his team of grave desecration. He eventually shut down excavations later that year and returned to London to collate the new tablets with those of previous digs. Smith was reconstructing one of the great libraries of antiquity, but tragically, he died of dysentery on the way to a third excavation in 1876. He was thirty-seven.

Smith's death left a significant vacuum. The British Museum scrambled to not only satisfy the appetites that Smith's discoveries created, but they also scrambled to appoint a capable scholar to take over his efforts. Yet as time would demonstrate, Smith, and the trailblazers that he represented, was never replaced despite the discovery of more tablets related to the Gilgamesh Epic and the flood account.

The Implications of the Gilgamesh Epic

The importance of the Gilgamesh Epic for understanding the Old Testament is unquestionably a comparative one. To be more precise, it illuminates the dynamics of the Old Testament as sacred literature, providing a valuable comparative tool for understanding the compositional realities of the Old Testament as well as its theology.

The History of the Gilgamesh Epic and the Implications for Textual Development

The history of the Gilgamesh Epic as a text begins with the Sumerians. In Sumer, a fragment of text was discovered that speaks of intercourse between King Lugalbana and the goddess Ninsun. While these two are known in later literary traditions to be the parents of Gilgamesh, Gilgamesh is not explicitly mentioned. Thus, any connection requires "a high degree of imagination."[13] Yet more certain is the independent existence of a handful of Sumerian poems that remember the exploits of Gilgamesh and were likely perpetuated for entertainment purposes.[14] Nevertheless, there is scant evidence that the Sumerians connected these traditions, although George does point to one textual fragment that speaks to the fusion of Gilgamesh's encounter with the netherworld with one of the poems that recount Gilgamesh's confrontation with Huwawa.[15] In the end, these Sumerian poems do bear witness to the "kernels" of the Gilgamesh Epic. As far back as Sumer, content existed that would become the backbone of the later editions of the Gilgamesh Epic.

Naturally, this raises the question regarding the process of how these independent traditions become compiled into the grand narrative that is the Gilgamesh Epic. To answer this, perhaps it is beneficial to start with the end of the historical process and work backward.

Tigay sums up the reality nicely.

> "When the epic was first unearthed in the mid-nineteenth century, the tablets discovered were from its latest, best-known version that of the first millennium BCE (often termed the "late" or "Standard Babylonian" version). Analysis of this version shows it to be, on the whole, coherent, integrated, and well structured. Still, enough inconsistences were noticeable for scholars to hypothesize about

13. George, *The Babylonian Gilgamesh Epic*, 5. George describes two others, both of which are problematic (pp. 5–7).

14. George, *The Babylonian Gilgamesh Epic*, 7. George acknowledges five, but Tigay is receptive to seven Sumerian compositions. Jeffrey H. Tigay, *The Evolution of the Gilgamesh Epic* (Wauconda, IL: Bolchazy-Carducci Publishers, 2002), 242.

15. George, *The Babylonian Gilgamesh Epic*, 16. Huwawa is a variation of the name Humbaba referenced above.

diverse origins for different parts of the epic. In subsequent decades, increasingly earlier forms of the epic and texts related to the
literary composition were discovered, until ultimately it became
possible to identify several different compositions which appeared
to have served as sources for the epic."

Integral to this process was the enigmatic priestly figure Sin-leqi-unninni.
According to a catalog list dating to the Neo-Assyrian period, the Gilgamesh
epic appears "according to the mouth" of Sin-leqi-unninni, a phrase widely
understood to denote authorship.[16] However, authorship in antiquity does
not assume modern connotations. Thus, the exact role of Sin-leqi-unninni
is difficult to determine. Nevertheless, as Tigay has concisely stated, it is
safe to assume that he "must have had some important, perhaps definitive,
contribution to its formulation."[17]

What is more definitive is that during the period just prior to the
Neo-Assyrian period, the Gilgamesh Epic exhibited an incredible amount
of popularity. Not only was there a proliferation of copies, as editions of the
narrative have been found all over the ancient Near East, but the Gilgamesh
Epic was translated into languages other than Akkadian and Sumerian. The
Hittite and Hurrian version are widely known, while an Elamite version is
hotly contested.[18] However, the most fascinating element of the narrative's
development during this period centers on the observable compositional
techniques employed by the scribes. Scholars recognize a diverse amount
of literary adaptation in this era, whether in the form of updating or reor-
ganizing of the narrative as well as simplifying or clarifying the language.
In fact, George has gone so far as to describe this period as a "mess."[19]
Consequently, it's difficult not to speculate that the standardization of the
Gilgamesh Epic that likely took place in the Neo-Assyrian period was an
endeavor that sought to combat this textual fluidity.

Yet the Old Babylonian Period was probably the most critical to the
development of the Gilgamesh Epic. However, it is also the most difficult to
reconstruct. Nevertheless, the textual remains are clear enough to demonstrate that the transition out of the Sumerian period saw the most important
steps in combining the once separated traditions. It appears that it was a
period characterized by scribal freedom and creativity. Bluntly stated, "In

16. George, *The Babylonian Gilgamesh Epic*, 28.

17. Tigay, *Evolution*, 245.

18. George, *The Babylonian Gilgamesh Epic*, 24.

19. George, *The Babylonian Gilgamesh Epic*, 27.

reworking the story of the hero Gilgamesh, the Babylonian poet did more than just adapt the traditional Sumerian literature."[20] For example, the literary tradition of a man brought up by wild animals, which is foundational to the Enkidu character, has no precedent in Sumerian literature, according to George.[21] Thus, the Old Babylonian author appears to have pulled from non-Sumerian literary traditions when developing Enkidu. Moreover, it was during the Old Babylonian period where Enkidu becomes more than merely a servant of Gilgamesh, becoming instead his "bosom friend."[22]

On the whole, then, the Old Babylonian period saw a shift—a narrative interested only in Gilgamesh became a narrative concerned with what could be gleaned from Gilgamesh's life. As stated by Tigay, the responsible party "realized that by judicious revision and integration of these sources he could tell an entertaining tale and at the same time explore these attitudes and make a statement about how one ought to live one's life knowing that death is inescapable. In doing so, this author created a new and profound work of art whose originality is in no way compromised by its indebtedness to earlier sources."[23]

In sum, the roots of the Gilgamesh Epic exist in Sumerian literature. However, it was during the Old Babylonian period when the Gilgamesh Epic took an integrated form that resembled the form of the Neo-Assyrian period. During the Middle Babylonian period, the popularity of the Epic exploded, which is evidenced in a textual proliferation. Fragments and copies have been found all over the ancient Near East and translations of the Epic have also been found. At some point, probably for reasons that sought militate against such a textual proliferation, the Epic was standardized.

So, what does this all mean? Why even discuss this reconstruction? While this discussion admittedly oversimplifies the development of the Gilgamesh Epic, the compositional process of the Gilgamesh Epic provides a comparative model for the Old Testament's process. For example, Tigay extensively details how small and large changes were made to the Gilgamesh Epic throughout its history of development.[24] Grammar was updated to reflect the changes in Akkadian. Also, outdated words were replaced, and entire phrases were added. Poetic lines were expanded

20. George, *The Babylonian Gilgamesh Epic*, 20.

21. George, *The Babylonian Gilgamesh Epic*, 20.

22. Tigay, *Evolution*, 53.

23. Tigay, *Evolution*, 54.

24. For a discussion, see Tigay, *Evolution*, 55–109.

or telescoped for a variety of reasons, and sometimes phrases were completely reformulated. In other words, the history of the Gilgamesh Epic is dotted with stylistic changes rooted in subjectivity, personal taste, or pragmatism. Nevertheless, they only minimally affected the most important semantics, and they certainly did not undermine the integrity of the text.[25] On the other hand, there were also larger-scale changes, such as the reorganization of entire sections, changes in characters, assimilation of scenes, and major additions, the most famous being the incorporation of the Deluge tradition and Tablet XII.

All of this sheds light on the conventions that stand behind many of the critical theories concerned with the composition of the Old Testament. For example, in the middle of the twentieth century, Martin Noth put for the idea of the Deuteronomistic History.[26] According to Noth, a historian compiled traditions and source material into a unified whole to explain the exile and destruction of Judah. While Noth's theory has been advanced and criticized,[27] the idea of a singular author creatively compiling a diverse set of material in a way that respects the integrity of each component while incorporating them into a unified whole compares to what is discernible within the Gilgamesh Epic.

In addition, the idea of large and small variations during the process of textual preservation is also widely recognized among biblical scholars. For example, Michael Fishbane has shown how specific grammatical features can signal the updating of a literary tradition.[28] Konrad Schmid has argued for the insertion of Deuteronomy in the context of a grand historical narrative that spanned from Exodus to Kings.[29] Countless examples could be invoked, but the point is simple. Ideas regarding the compositional history of the Old Testament are not the ramblings of scholars that seek to undermine the integrity of the Old Testament. Rather, such ideas are built upon widely attested ancient literary conventions.

25. Tigay, *Evolution*, 71.

26. Martin Noth, *The Deuteronomistic History* (JSOTSup 15; Sheffield: JSOT Press, 1991).

27. For a concise view of the contours, see Sandra Richter, "Deuteronomistic History," in the *Dictionary of the Old Testament Historical Books* (eds. Bill T. Arnold and Hugh Williamson; Downers Grove: InterVarsity Press, 2005), 219–30.

28. Michael Fishbane, *Biblical Interpretation in Ancient Israel* (Oxford: Clarendon Press, 1988), 44–65.

29. Konard Schmid, *Genesis and the Moses Story: Israel's Dual Origins in the Hebrew Bible* (trans. James D. Nogalski; Siphrut 3; Winona Lake, IN: Eisenbrauns, 2010), 346.

However, the analogy that I am discussing here is not perfect. The Gilgamesh Epic enjoys a rich catalog of extant texts that testify to the phases of development. Stated otherwise, the Gilgamesh Epic enjoys empirical evidence that can be evaluated while the Old Testament largely relies upon reconstruction and circumstantial evidence. This is a legitimate criticism of the analogy. Nevertheless, the evidence of Qumran is worth mentioning at this point. Not to anticipate a later chapter too much, the Dead Sea Scrolls testify to a textual fluidity around the traditions of the Old Testament during the first century CE. Moreover, scrolls and scroll fragments, particularly of Jeremiah and Daniel, attest to reordered and markedly different editions of Jeremiah and Daniel than what one sees in the Protestant Old Testament. Thus, the Dead Sea Scrolls put the notion of a compositional history beyond question and on firm ground. By implication, there is legitimate reason to pursue textual reconstruction in order to understand as much as possible about the textual history of the Old Testament.

Understanding the Significance of the Old Testament's Theology

When it comes to understanding the comparative implications of the Gilgamesh Epic vis-à-vis the theology of the Old Testament, numerous angles can be taken. For example, one can analyze the character of the gods by means of their actions. One can also look into the differing views of the afterlife and the expectations surrounding those that have passed on. However, and at the chance of sounding glib, I will limit my discussions to two topics.

In 2015, Laura Feldt published an informative essay on the concept of wilderness in Old Babylonian literature.[30] She argued that the perceptions of the wilderness were not simplistic. Rather, Mesopotamian perceptions were nuanced and complicated, perhaps even ambiguous. The wilderness regions were not understood to be completely diabolical, but rather dangerously necessary. In constructing this thesis, one of the texts Feldt analyzed was the Old Babylonian tradition of Gilgamesh versus Huwawa. While I have discussed the reality that the Old Babylonian version of the Gilgamesh traditions were not identical to the Standard Babylonian version, the most salient points that arise from Feldt's discussion apply to this task.

---

30. Laura Feldt, "Religion, Nature, and Ambiguous Space in Ancient Mesopotamia: The Mountain Wilderness in Old Babylonian Religious Narratives," *Numen* 63 (2015): 1–36.

First, Feldt emphasizes that the collision of Gilgamesh, Enkidu, and Huwawa is a combat narrative, which often pits a hero against a prominent foe.[31] Yet progressing further, she also argues that it's ultimately a discussion on the principles of cosmic order and the mutual interplay between different elements within society.[32] Second, the wilderness is a place of great transgression that produces lasting effects. According tablets II and III of the Gilgamesh Epic, Gilgamesh and Enkidu ignored several warnings. Thus, the death of Enkidu was the result of the duo's cavalier exploits. Third, Huwawa's function as the guardian of the Cedar Forest was a part of cosmic order. And given that Huwawa's presence was sanctioned by the gods, the endeavors of Gilgamesh and Enkidu upset that balance. Fourth, the resources of the wilderness were necessary for the perpetuation of a well-cultured society. The cedars of the Cedar Forest were valued in construction and existed as a symbol of prosperity. In other words, the wilderness simultaneously repulses and attracts people.

All things considered, Feldt makes a compelling argument for the complexity surrounding the wilderness in the Mesopotamian mind. Similarly, the wilderness concept according to the Old Testament is intricate and nuanced.[33] The wilderness is where Israel encountered the Lord at Sinai, but also the death of an entire generation. It was the context of Israel's salvation at the Sea of Reeds (Exod 14) as well as the Baal Peor episode (Numb 25:1–15). It was the place of God's miraculous provision through manna and quail, but also Israel's most intense grumbling and testing. In short, the wilderness was where Israel experienced some of its highest highs and lowest lows.

But what is perhaps most interesting is the parallel that the wilderness is the place of great transgression that led to one of the biggest scars on the psyches of Gilgamesh and Israel respectively. For Gilgamesh, it was where the fate of Enkidu was sealed. For Israel, it would become a painful and nostalgic and educational memory. Yet even among this convergence of ideas, the uniqueness of the Israelite perception can still be observed. The Old Testament shows that Israel's understanding of the wilderness was profoundly shaped by its covenant with the Lord. The wilderness was the context necessary for forging that fledgling relationship, and the

31. Feldt, "Ambiguous Space," 12.

32. Feldt, "Ambiguous Space," 14.

33. See David B. Schreiner, "Wilderness, Theology of," in the *Global Wesleyan Dictionary of Biblical Theology* (Kansas City: The Foundry), forthcoming.

tragedies experienced there were in response to conscious infractions of that agreement. In other words, it did not have to be one of the most painful experiences in Israel's history. In addition, within the Gilgamesh Epic, the wilderness is the place to pursue fame and reputation, the promotion of selfish ambition. In contrast, the wilderness in the Old Testament was where a corporate religious identity was forged.

When George Smith first published his discovery of Tablet XI, one's understanding of Israel's thought-world was taken to new heights. Smith showed that within the Gilgamesh Epic there was an account of a massive, divinely sanctioned deluge that almost eradicated humanity. Humanity's continuation was due to the salvation of a relatively small number of humans and animals by means of boat. Yet the similarities go beyond generic similarities. In both accounts, attention is given to the construction of the boat. Moreover, the flood was said to be the result of conscious decisions made by the deity(ies) in charge. After the flood subsided, both accounts detail critical sacrifices performed by the survivors as well as the presentation of a "sign" as commemoration of the event. There is also the similarity of the boat coming to rest upon a mountain top as the waters receded and the releasing of doves and ravens to determine the level of the water.

Despite these points of contact, there are numerous differences as well.

- First, and most obviously, the Gilgamesh Epic assumes a polytheistic worldview and the biblical account a monotheistic one. This has tremendous implications for the tone and atmosphere of each narrative. For example, the Gilgamesh Epic describes a pantheon populated by ambitious deities. Ea undermines the intentions of the other gods by alerting Utnapishtum to the deluge. Later, Ea must issue a statement (arguing his case) before Enlil, who is surprised and angry that humanity survived.

- Second, according to the Gilgamesh Epic, we are not sure why the flood occurs. Yet the biblical account explicitly states that the Lord has chosen to send a flood due to the perpetual immorality and unrighteousness of humanity. Similarly, we are not told why Utnapishtum was privy to the plan. For Noah, he was righteous.

- Third, the reactions of the gods in the Gilgamesh Epic stand in stark contrast to the demeanor of the Lord. The Mesopotamian gods are shocked, frightened, and lose their minds. In contrast, the characterization of Yahweh is cool, calculated, and always in control.

- Fourth, the mentioning of Shuruppak sets the narrative in an urban context. The biblical account does not concern itself with such a contextualization.

- Fifth, both accounts admit that the relationship between humanity and the gods is difficult at times, but the difficulties between Yahweh and his creation are rooted in the sinfulness of humanity. Conversely, the attitudes of the Mesopotamian gods seem arbitrary, even born out of selfishness.

- Sixth, Utnapishtum is conspiratorial. He dupes people into to helping him by saying that "cake from heaven" would fall as soon as he left. In the biblical account, attention is given only to Noah and his family and they must accomplish their task in isolation.

- Seventh, Utnapishtum brings riches and craftsmen on the boat, along with the animals. In the biblical account, salvation belongs solely to

Noah's family, suggesting that the biblical account is solely concerned with the preservation of life and not any cultural continuity between pre and post-diluvian ages.

Consequently, it would be an understatement to merely say that Israel was influenced by its larger cultural milieu. To be more precise, the Gilgamesh Epic demonstrates that Israel shared an entire thought-world with its larger milieu, discussing the realities of human existence in remarkably similar ways. Motifs, perceptions, concepts, and other literary and cognitive concepts were shared. Yet what made Israel unique was its revolutionary belief system that was rooted in the idea that a singular God would construct a covenantal relationship with them. This becomes crystal clear when comparing the theology of the Old Testament with the theology of the Gilgamesh Epic.

4

Ugarit

Anyone familiar with the Old Testament, particularly the Historical Books, will likely recognize the names Baal and Asherah. There is the classic confrontation in 1 Kings 18 when the prophet Elijah squares off against 450 prophets of Baal to determine which god is legitimate and which is a phony. Deuteronomy rails against the pitfalls of idolatry and even calls for the destruction of asherah poles (Deut 12:3). Dagon is familiar with those who know the narratives of 1 Samuel 4–7. However, before the later portion of the 1920's our understanding of these deities, and Canaanite religion for that matter, was remarkably limited. All this changed when a farmer, minding his own business as he suffered through the daily grind, struck a large stone with his plow.

Ras Shamra: Ugarit[1]

The year was 1928, and the story goes that a farmer was innocently plowing a field near the bay of Minet el-Beida, near Latakia, Syria. His plow struck a large stone situated just below the surface, and upon a brief investigation he realized that the stone was man made. Naturally, his curiosity took over, and he looked a little more intently. When he did, he found that this stone marked a tunnel that led further into the earth. At the tunnel's end was a tomb that contained items of significant value. Consequently, the farmer helped himself to a few items in order to make a buck or two on the antiquities market.

---

1. The following summary is indebted to Yon's survey of the site, as well the summary of Craigie. See Peter C. Craigie, *Ugarit and the Old Testament* (Grand Rapids: William B. Eerdmans, 1983); Marguerite Yon, *The City of Ugarit at Tell Ras Shamra* (Winona Lake, IN: Eisenbrauns, 2006).

At the time, the region was under French control due to several post World War I agreements. So, when the farmer's newly found treasures hit the market, it was only a matter of time before the French authorities would receive word. Eventually, Charles Virolleaud was notified, and he in turn dispatched one of his assistants to give a report. That report mentioned Minet el-Beida and even the nearby tel Ras Shamra. However, as the story goes, his report was rather underwhelming and lackluster. Nevertheless, a more detailed investigated ensued thanks in large part to the intuition of several important people. Minet el-Beida exhibited an obvious strategic value, and local tradition had linked the area to treasure and a few notable legends. Sometimes common sense and local lore are the best encouragement for archaeologists.

Eventually, plans were drafted, and approval was given to subject the newly found tomb to systematic excavations. Claude F. A. Schaeffer was tapped to lead the excavation team in 1929, but apparently there was tension on the ground. In a way that conjures up images of Neh 4:17–18, a small military detachment was dispatched with the excavation team to provide protection as they conducted their daily business. Yet despite the circumstances, the payoff was essentially immediate. Idols, ceramics, weapons, decorated weapons, and all types of precious finds were excavated at incredible speed. Moreover, Schaeffer quickly determined that the tombs of Minet el-Beida were royal tombs. Ironically, however, Minet el-Beida was not the prized site in the region. That would be a title reserved for the nearby tel Ras Shamra, or ancient Ugarit.

Meaning "fennel hill," René Dussard had encouraged Schaeffer to pursue excavations there. The tel sits less than a mile inland from the bay of Minet el-Beida, and it's bordered by two seasonal rivers to the north and the south. Around the tel there is a "large, fertile, and fairly well irrigated plain," but to the east there is a mountain range that provides a natural border and shield from the harsh desert interior.[2] Consequently, Ras Shamra enjoys a pleasant Mediterranean climate. In fact, Marguerite Yon has claimed that Ras Shamra's climate was one of the driving factors in the development of Ugarit's "Golden Age."[3]

Like Minet el-Beida, excavations were immediately successful. Decorated weapons, monuments dedicated to various deities, and sophisticated architecture were some of the first finds. The most difficult thing about the

2. Yon, *The City of Ugarit*, 10.
3. Yon, *The City of Ugarit*, 13–14.

initial excavations at Ras Shamra was deciding where to dig. Initially the highest point on the tel was chosen, which turned out to be the acropolis. From there, the northeast corner of the tel was excavated as it exhibited visible architecture remnants, not to mention that local traditions pointed to it as strategically important. In the end, such decisions paid off quickly. Neither the excavators nor the interested public had to wait long to see the value of Ras Shamra. Palaces, temples, and complicated city planning was observed very quickly. But without a doubt, the most impactful find of the initial excavations was a high priest's library (see below).

While only a fraction of the tel has been systematically been excavated, excavations have been substantial enough to allow for the identification of sectors within the city. Excavators speak of the royal zone, the acropolis, the south acropolis, the eastern and western lower city, the city center, the residential quarter, the south city, and others. What's more, the architecture of the city shows "large, luxurious homes standing beside more modest homes . . . adjoining non-residential buildings such as temples or shops."[4] Houses varied in shape and size, between 80 to 800 square meters. Cumulatively, these realities "bear witness to a thriving city with a variety of structures."[5] Ugarit was "a densely inhabited city where private residents found refuge at the end of narrow streets. They city had no regular layout, because it was the outgrowth of many centuries of continual reconstruction on the same spot."[6]

Ugarit was dominated by its royal precincts and the acropolis. The so-called "royal zone" covers over 10,000 square meters, but it does appear that it was demarcated from the rest of the city. According to Yon, the royal zone was "reserved for palace activities,"[7] and it even had its own sewer system. The palace itself, which came to be a focal point of the royal zone, was approximately 7,000 square meters and represents one of the most formidable and complex structures in antiquity.

4. Yon, *The City of Ugarit*, 29.
5. Yon, *The City of Ugarit*, 28–29.
6. Yon, *The City of Ugarit*, 29.
7. Yon, *The City of Ugarit*, 34–35.

Accessed on the west by a royal plaza, the structure is a labyrinth of rooms that also testifies to the structure's several phases of development. The 10+ staircases testify to the presence of multiple floors for the palace, and there were several gardens and courtyards also discovered. Notably, there were also several archives discovered on the premises, all of which have allowed scholars to reconstruct daily life and the administrative tendencies of the royal family.

Outside the palace, but still within the royal zone, excavators identified other important installations, including guard posts, temples, smaller palaces, and various other buildings. Immediately to the north and east of the royal zone is another sector that showed association with the city's elite. There, the excavators unearthed other significant installations, all of which have been identified in various ways. For example, there is another palace, the likely residence of the Queen Mother, and several prominent plazas. As for the acropolis, it dominates the tel and sits east of the royal palace. A temple to Baal and Dagon, both of which were built to the same floor plan, existed there. They were large temples set off by notations of sacred space. Inside, finds of all shapes and sizes were excavated. In Baal's temple two famous steles were found, including one of Baal with an outstretched arm holding a lightning bolt. In Dagon's temple, a dedicatory inscription was found, but there is evidence both temples were also home to the worship to many other gods and goddesses.

⟶ There were several buildings between the temples to Baal and Dagon, and they appear to have been connected by a prominent street. One of those buildings was a treasure trove of cuneiform texts. It's been called the House of the High Priest. Numerous decorated and dedicated weapons, various bronze tools, basic utensils, and a hoard of cuneiform texts were discovered there. The importance of these texts is their mythological and religious quality. Whereas so many of the texts discovered throughout Ras Shamra are administrative in nature, thus critical for the reconstruction of daily life, the texts of the High Priest speak to the religious ideology of the city. In these texts one reads about Baal, El, Anat, Mot, Yamm and the rest of the Canaanite pantheon. Moreover, one reads about the greats of Canaanite lore, such as King Keret, Danel, Aqhat, and more.

The history of occupation at Ras Shamra extends from the Neolithic period to the Roman period. However, the occupation of the tel during the Late Bronze Age marks the apex of its history. The occupations during the Persian and Roman periods pale in comparison. But during the Bronze Ages, with a series of occupational ebbs and flows notwithstanding, the city hit its stride. The Early Bronze Age occupation shows the first signs of urbanization, only to see it collapse very violently and very enigmatically at the end of the third millennium. Such a cycle, however, is typical of the age. In the Middle Bronze Age, there was significant occupation at the tel but not to the level of the Early Bronze Age. But with the onset of the Late Bronze Age, Ugarit became one of the most influential and cosmopolitan cities of in the Mediterranean basin.

The Golden Age of Ugarit began in the fourteenth or thirteenth century. During this time, the city controlled a territory of approximately 1300 square miles, making a small but influential kingdom.[8] Nevertheless, the kingdom was restricted by the two superpowers of the era: Egypt to the south and Hatti to the north. Both were ambitious and sought to control the critical land bridge of Syria-Palestine. This ensured that Ugarit was constantly in the cross-hairs of imperial ambition. In fact, there is evidence to suggest that prior to the campaigns of the Hittite King Suppiluliuma around 1350 BCE, Ugarit was a vassal city to the Egyptian Empire. It became a vassal to the Hittites after the Hittite king campaigned against Mitanni and its Syrian vassals.[9] Yet in the end, Ugarit played its part well. It reaped the rewards of the economic system that defined the Late Bronze Age, functioning as a critical sea port for the exchange of goods throughout the Mediterranean basin and the Fertile Crescent. Trade, agricultural, and industry defined the kingdom's economic portfolio, all of which translated into one of the most affluent and advanced cities in antiquity.

Shockingly, all of this came crashing down with the collapse of the Late Bronze Age, which also happens to be one of the great mysteries of

8. Craigie, *Ugarit and the Old Testament*, 27–28.

9. Yon, *The City of Ugarit*, 19–20.

ancient history. Whatever the cause, the result was clear enough. The global economic and political systems that connected the cultures of Greece, the Mediterranean, Egypt, Syria-Palestine, and the Fertile Crescent were gone. Some kingdoms, such as the Hittites and Ugarit effectively ceased to exist, and others were reduced to a shell of themselves, such as Egypt.

Similar to Mari, the excavations at Ras Shamra have spanned decades and multiple directors. Schaeffer headed excavations until 1939 when the events of World War II suspended excavations. They resumed in 1948 with Schaeffer still at the helm, but in 1972 leadership was assumed by de Contenson in 1972 and then by Margueron in 1975. In 1978 Marguerite Yon took over excavations until 1998, when the excavations shifted from a French affair to a joint Franco-Syrian one. Yves Calvet and Bassam Jamous became co-directors. In 2005, Jamal Haïdar replaced Jamous when he became Director of Antiquities.

The Implications of Ugarit

In 1983, Peter Craigie discussed the "gaps" that separate the modern reader of the Old Testament from the world of the Old Testament. Craigie claimed, "If no attempt is made to bridge those gaps, then the lack of familiarity with biblical language and culture will contribute to a failure to understand the biblical message."[10] But to be sure, these gaps are not the fault of the text or the author for that matter—as if they forgot to mention some important detail. Rather, the onus is upon the modern reader to "remedy the deficiency" so that understanding can be maximized.[11] This is where Ugarit comes into play. The evidence at ancient Ugarit allows the modern reader to fill in the gaps in their knowledge of biblical history and ancient Near Eastern culture so that important realities can be recognized and appropriated during the interpretive process. The value of Ugarit, therefore, is foremost a comparative one.

But the implications of Ugarit are more specific than just being comparative. At least four categories of insight associated with the excavations at Ras Shamra have proven to be radical for understanding the Old Testament: 1) its witness to the collapse of the Late Bronze Age; 2) its witness to Canaanite religion; 3) its illumination of Old Testament poetry; 4) miscellaneous points of clarification.

10. Craigie, *Ugarit and the Old Testament*, 3–4.
11. Craigie, *Ugarit and the Old Testament*, 5.

Yet before any discussion happens, it's worthwhile to emphasize the textual footprint of ancient Ugarit. So much of what's exciting about ancient Ugarit goes back, in one way or another, to the textual hoards unearthed during the decades of excavation. And make no mistake, that hoard is large. Thousands of tablets have been unearthed, and they bear witness to many things, from daily activities to ideology. But all the tablets would be mere paperweights if it were not for a small group of inquisitive and creative men who deciphered Ugaritic, the language of Ugarit.

It was clear early in the excavations that several languages were used in Ugarit's records and literature. They included Akkadian, Hurrian, Egyptian, Hittite, Cypro-Minoan, and Sumerian. Yet among these languages, there was one that stood out as it seemed to repeat a small set of cuneiform symbols. Upon closer examination, linguists eventually concluded that the recurring wedge-shaped symbols were not indicative of a syllabic writing system, like that of Akkadian. Rather, it was indicative of a 30-symbol alphabetic system. And most exciting of all was the fact that this system was unknown at that point! Ugarit boasted its own language, and the hoard of texts offered scholars a critical context to decipher and understand a new language!

The decipherment of Ugaritic is largely the result of three people who worked independently but took ques from the published research of the others. Charles Virolleaud, Hans Bauer, and Edouard Dhorme all had a role to play in the decipherment of Ugaritic.[12] Most impressively, in approximately 1.5 years after the discovery of the textual archives Ugaritic was deciphered.

Ugarit and the Collapse of the Late Bronze Age

Ugarit provides an invaluable witness to the end of the Late Bronze Age. Eric Cline has recently reconstructed the collapse of the economic and political system that dominated the Mediterranean basin and the ancient Near East during the Late Bronze Age.[13] In doing so, he shed light on the importance of Ugarit. According to Cline, Ugarit was an "international entrepôt." The sheer volume of shipping lists, product catalogs, taxation lists, negotiations, and various official correspondences between the major imperial powers of the day point to Ugarit as a critical choke point in this economic system.[14] For example, texts list perishable exports going through Ugarit to Assyria that originated at various places throughout the Mediterranean basin. Some texts found in the House of Rapanu detail negotiations between the king of Carchemish and the Egyptians. Elsewhere, from the House of Urtenu, texts show how members of Ugarit's populace were involved in brokering and/or documenting trade deals and other international affairs. Consequently, the textual evidence of Ugarit paints a picture not only of Ugarit during the Late Bronze Age, but also how the city functioned within a very prosperous and globalized system. Ugarit was a focal point, and the system in which it operated was complex and lucrative.

Yet the lucrative system came to a violent end, and Ugarit also bears witness to this unexpected system-collapse. Sometime between 1190 and 1185 BCE, during the reign of King Ammurapi, Ugarit was put under immense pressure that ultimately led to the destruction of the city. While the exact details of the city's collapse are still debated, the archaeological

12. See Craigie, *Ugarit and the Old Testament*, 15–21 for a description of the methods used by each party.

13. Eric H. Cline, *1177 B.C.: The Year Civilization Collapsed* (Princeton: Princeton University Press, 2014). For more details, see Cline's discussion.

14. Cline, *1147 B.C.*, 102–08.

evidence points to a quick and violent end. Massive destruction layers, collapsed walls, broken vessels, and more characterize Ras Shamra's stratum III. In addition, there is indisputable evidence that the city was abandoned for centuries after this event, remaining uninhabited until the Persian period. Even then, it never regained its Late Bronze Age glory.

The collapse of Ugarit at the end of the Late Bronze Age is one piece in a very complicated and enigmatic picture. Certainly, the Late Bronze Age collapse was not the result of any singular cause. Rather, it's proper to speak of a "perfect storm," whereby one issue compounded the effects of another until a turn of events could not be stopped. Yet while the causes are mysterious, the effect of the collapse is clear enough. The economic and imperial system that dominated the Mediterranean basin and the ancient Near East, a system that allowed certain groups to reach levels of power and influence unprecedented at that time, was gone. And in its wake, a significant sociopolitical vacuum was left. The region of Canaan was ripe for the picking, and into this vacuum both Israel and the Philistines would step.

The Canaanite Religious System

The texts of ancient Ugarit have been revolutionary for our understanding of the Canaanite religious system. Prior to the textual discoveries of Ugarit, information on the Canaanite religious system came from the Old Testament. Obviously, such a scenario was less than ideal, particularly in light of the Old Testament's polemical posture toward Canaanite religion. With Ugarit, however, scholars can reconstruct and investigate the Canaanite pantheon, read about the mythical exploits of the deities, even reconstruct certain rituals and divination practices.[15] For example, an atonement ritual has been discovered. This ritual contains at least 5 sections that disclose the type of animal to be offered, the infraction committed, and the party that will receive atonement. The following is an excerpt from KTU 1.40.[16]

> "Now we present a donkey for purification, for purification of the men of Ugarit, and atonement for the foreigner within Ugarit, and atonement for Yaman, and atonement for ʿrmt, and atonement for Ugarit, and atonement for Niqmad.

15. For a useful survey of the content and importance of the religious texts at ancient Ugarit, see Pierre Bordreuil and Dennis Pardee, "Ugarit: Texts and Literature," *ABD*: 6:706–21.

16. Nicolas Wyatt, *Religious Texts from Ugarit* (2d ed.; Sheffield: Sheffield Academic Press, 2002), 345–46.

Whenever your state of grace be changed, whether by accusation of the Qatians, or by the accusation of the Dadmians, or by
the accusation of the Hurrians, or by the accusation of the Hittites,
or by the accusation of the Cypriots, or by the accusation of gbr, or
by accusation of your oppressed ones, or by the accusation of your
poor, or by the accusation of qrbzl, whenever your state of grace be
changed, either through your anger, or through your impatience,
or through some evil that you have done; whenever your state of
grace be changed concerning the sacrifices and the offering, our
sacrifice we offer: this is the offering that we make, this is the vic-
tim that we immolate.

May it be borne aloft to the father of the gods, may it be borne
aloft to the pantheon of the gods, to the assembly of the gods, to
Thukamun and Shanim, here is the donkey."

Such a ritual conjures up Leviticus, particularly the Day of Atonement
ritual in chapter 16. However, caution must be encouraged. In this case,
the dynamics of any literary relationship, if there is even any relationship
at all, are not immediately clear. As will be discussed below, one should be
cautious in pursuing or over extending any potential literary relationship.
What is clear is that this text is duplicated elsewhere in the textual archives
of Ugarit,[17] which has caused some scholars to propose that this atonement
ritual was broadly practiced.[18]

In addition, models of livers, a model of a lung, and other physi-
ological models have also been discovered. They demonstrate the role of
extispicy and other forms of divination in the Canaanite religious system.
Consider this. One Ugaritic text catalogs how certain birth defects, likely
on a cow, are omens for the future.

"And (if) [it] has no right ear, [the enemy will] devastate the land

[. . . and will] consume it.

And (if) [it] has no left ear, the king [will] devastate the land of
[his] enemy

and will consume it."[19]

17. Wyatt, *Religious Texts*, 341–42.

18. Bordreuil and Pardee, "Ugarit: Texts and Literature," 6:709.

19. "A Text for Diving by Misformed Births of Sheep and Goats," translated by Dennis
Pardee (*COS*, 1:90, ll. 35–38). Also see Pierre Bordreuil and Dennis Pardee, *A Manual of
Ugaritic* (LSAWS 3; Winona Lake, IN: Eisenbrauns, 2009), 226–32.

Most famously, the texts of ancient Ugarit have given several lengthy myths that highlight the exploits of humanity and the pantheon. The Kirta Epic addresses concerns of the monarchal institution. More precisely, the epic discusses issues that threaten the vitality and longevity of a royal line, including dynastic succession and progeny, illness, and deposition.[20] The tale of Aqhat is more elusive than Kirta's narrative, but it is similar in that it addresses issues of survival and the role that the deities play in the process.[21] Unfortunately, both texts are extremely fragmentary, which alludes to a prudent rule of thumb when dealing with any Ugaritic text. Due to the fragmentary nature of so many of them, all conclusions should remain tentative.

The Baal Cycle was also found at Ugarit. This text, more famous than Kirta or Aqhat's stories, details the exploits of Baal vis-à-vis other deities in the Canaanite pantheon, including El, Yamm, and Mot. According to the text, Baal defeats Yamm, then receives a palace, but is then defeated by Mot. This text, perhaps more than any other, opened a new world to understanding the Canaanite religious system. No longer were scholars restricted by a single source that was hostile to Baal, Asherah, El, and the other pagan deities of its day.

It also opened new lines of inquiry. For example, in 1971 J. C. de Moor articulated the theory that the exploits of Baal, who is the storm and fertility god, recounted in the Baal Cycle mirror the agricultural cycles of the world.[22] That is, Baal's life as detailed in the Baal Cycle was cyclical just as the cycles of the seasons are cyclical. However, de Moor's ideas have been criticized from several angles, particularly since his chief theory requires a reordering of the narrative from what appears in the textual evidence from Ugarit.[23] One must concede that it's also possible that the Baal cycle was composed more to glorify Baal than to discuss the agricultural cycle of a normal year.[24] Similarly, the relationship between deities in

20. Kenton L. Sparks, *Ancient Texts for the Study of the Hebrew Bible: A Guide to the Background Literature* (Peabody, MA: Hendrickson Publishers, 2005), 293–94

21. For a brief discussion of the possibilities for purpose as well as a bibliography, see Sparks, *Ancient Texts*, 294–96.

22. J. C. de Moor, *The Seasonal Pattern in the Ugaritic Myth of Ba'lu* (AOAT 16; Neukirchen: Vluyn, 1971).

23. John Day, "Baal (Deity)," *ABD*, 1:546.

24. Day rightly points to the obvious agricultural metaphors at strategic points in the narrative. Thus, "It would be incorrect, however, to reject all seasonal elements in the work." "Baal (Deity)," 1:546.

the Canaanite pantheon is not quite clear.[25] Day notes that it's not certain if there is a tension between Baal and El, and there is also a debate over Baal's lineage. Also, when it comes to Baal's relationship with Asherah, whom the Old Testament often pairs with Baal, the Ugaritic texts are not clear. Consequently, while the mythical texts, alongside with various cultic texts, have given valuable insight into the thought world of the Canaanite religious system, questions remain. Moreover, one must remember that definitely describing any ancient "thought world" is notoriously difficult. And at a place like Ugarit, which was so cosmopolitan and transitory, that difficulty is only increased.[26]

Understanding Biblical Hebrew Poetry

The Ugaritic texts have offered an invaluable tool for understanding the dynamics of Biblical Hebrew poetry. From conceptual parallels, to syntactical agreement, to parallelism in general as a poetic device, the texts of ancient Ugarit offer an expansive corpus that exhibits overwhelming overlap with the poetry of the Old Testament. Put succinctly, "It is fair to say that Hebrew and Ugaritic poets employed the same basic structures and conventions."[27] In fact, Mitchell Dahood's influential commentary on the Psalms explored the immense possibilities when one reads the Psalms with an awareness of the Ugaritic texts—although Dahood's work has been criticized as a chief example of parallelomania.[28]

Psalm 29 provides a great example into the insights and pitfalls related to reading Old Testament poetry in light of Ugaritic texts. In 1935, Harold Ginsberg proposed that Psalm 29 was a psalm adapted from a hymn composed to Baal.[29] Ginsberg noted certain ideas in the psalm that had a palpable pagan flare to them (cf. Ps 29:3–5). Also, there are the geographic references to Lebanon, Tyre, Sidon, Kadesh, and northern forests. Most importantly, Ginsberg pointed out that the final verses of the psalm echoed

25. "Baal (Deity)," 1:546–47.

26. Michael Williams, *Basics of Ancient Ugaritic: A Concise Grammar, Workbook, and Lexicon* (Grand Rapids: Zondervan, 2012), 24–25.

27. Craigie, *Ugarit and the Old Testament*, 24–25.

28. Mitchell Dahood, *Psalms* (ABC 16; Garden City, NJ: Double Day, 1966–70; Reprint Yale University Press, 1995).

29. Harold L. Ginsberg, "A Phoenician Hymn in the Psalter" in *Atti del XIX Congresso Internazionale degli Orientalisti* (Rome: Tipografia del Senato, 1938), 472–76.

praises leveled at Baal. Together, this was enough for him to suggest a Yahwization of a pagan psalm.

Ginsberg's thesis was accepted by many and further developed. For instance, in 1950, Frank Moore Cross investigated Psalm 29 in light of what could be determined about *Canaanite* poetry.[30] Nevertheless, one must be diligent in where the evidence takes us.[31] Craigie is correct to note that it's hard not to see Psalm 29 as evidence that the biblical writers gained inspiration from popular culture.[32] Psalm 29 was not composed in a vacuum. Moreover, it's difficult not to allow for the possibility that a biblical writer may have adapted, or Yahwehized, a pagan hymn. Yet one must also not allow any historical possibility to undermine any theological value, as if history is the absolute driving force of theology. Our focus must move beyond the mechanisms that may have produced the psalm. And to take it a step further, any historical possibility must be considered in the framework of how it may augment a text's theology. In the case of Ps 29, if a Canaanite origin is correct, then it may be best to see it as a testament to how the truth of God can be redeemed out of a pagan context and clarified in an orthodox manner.

Miscellaneous Points of Clarification

The Ugaritic texts have also allowed an understanding of some enigmatic statements within the Old Testament. Just a few will suffice.

- One of the words used in the Old Testament for God is El (אֵל), who is one of the chief gods of the Canaanite pantheon. Moreover, as is discussed elsewhere in this work, the Lord has been associated in certain Hebrew inscriptions with Asherah, another deity in the Canaanite pantheon. Therefore, it seems prudent to admit that there was some cross-pollination between Canaanite and Israelite religion. Meaning, investigations into Canaanite religion have and will likely continue to provide insight into the development of Israelite religion.

30. Frank Moore Cross, "Notes on a Canaanite Psalm in the Old Testament," *BASOR* 117 (1950): 19–21.

31. For a critical assessment of this thesis, see Peter Craigie, *Psalms 1–50* (WBC 19; 2d ed.; Nashville: Thomas Nelson, 2004), 243–46.

32. Craigie, *Ugarit and the Old Testament*, 70–72.

- Baal is described throughout the Ugaritic texts as one who "rides on the clouds," which is also a title ascribed to the Lord in various locations and in various ways (cf. Deut 33:26; Is 19:1; Ps 68:4, 33). But in Daniel 7, an awareness of the Ugaritic imagery becomes particularly fascinating. If Heiser is right, the Ugaritic echoes of Daniel add a rich depth to the Bible's Trinitarian theology.[33]

- The prophet Amos is introduced in 1:1 as one who was "among the shepherds of Tekoa" (NRSV). The word is *nōqēd* (נֹקֵד), which also appears in a few Ugaritic texts. In one location, Ilimilku is labeled as a *nōqēd* while being described as a chief among the priests.[34] Thus, some have suggested that Amos's original occupation was associated with the priestly establishment of Jerusalem. However, when one considers the entire semantic field, it's best to understand Amos as a manger and marketer of large herds of sheep.[35] He was a person of high social status and not some lowly individual farmer.

- In Jer 16:5 and Amos 6:7 the noun *marzēaḥ* (מַרְזֵחַ) is used. Jeremiah is instructed not to enter into a "house of mourning" (NRSV) in light of the pending exile, and Amos announces how the disconnected affluent of society will be the first to head into exile, which will silence the "revelry of the loungers" (NRSV). The same word appears in some Ugaritic texts, and it may be associated with elements of pagan worship. While not definitive, is it possible that the prophets are alluding to such associations?

- The concoction of figs *dᵉbelet tᵉʾēnim* (דְּבֶלֶת תְּאֵנִים) applied to Hezekiah's deadly boil (2 Kgs 20:7; Is 38:21) appears in some notable medical texts. In one text, "an aged bunch of figs" (*dblt*) is to be applied with raisins and flour to the nostrils of a horse if it is found to "suffer in the head and is utterly prostrate."[36]

In closing, it's worth reiterating that the importance of Ugarit is largely a comparative one, and at the center of it are its texts. Those texts tell us about Canaanite religion and Bronze Age culture. In the words of Christopher Hays, the texts allow the biblical interpreter to obtain a certain level

---

33. Michael Heiser, "What's Ugaritic Got to Do with Anything?" *Logos Bible Software*, https://www.logos.com/ugaritic (accessed on January 1, 2019).

34. Wyatt, *Religious Texts*, 147.

35. Craigie, *Ugarit and the Old Testament*, 71–73.

36. Bordreuil and Pardee, *A Manual of Ugaritic*, 224.

of "cultural literacy."[37] But as with any comparative tool, it can go sideways without the proper methodological constraints. Ugarit was geographically close to the land of ancient Israel, and its language is a part of the Northwest Semitic dialects (of which Biblical Hebrew is also a member). Yet Ugarit was a Bronze Age city, and Israel did not establish itself in the region until the Iron Age. Moreover, Canaanite and Israelite theology diverged at critical points. Consequently, when looking to Ugarit for clarification or fresh insight, a critical and balanced posture is necessary.

37. Hays, *Hidden Riches*, 3.

5

The Dead Sea Scrolls

It's not often that you can say that something in Biblical Studies is cinema worthy. Moreover, it's difficult to make a case for the production of a documentary when it comes to issues of Biblical Studies. The truth is that the issues of Biblical Studies appeal only to a few. But when it comes to the discovery and publication of the Dead Sea Scrolls, you could make a compelling case for some type of cinematic production. It involves questionable business dealings, perceived scholarly conspiracies, and ingenuous defiance. And to put icing on the cake, the implications of the Dead Sea Scrolls have been nothing short of paradigm shifting. The scrolls have impacted the discipline of textual criticism as well as our awareness of the diversity of first century Judaism and the complexity of the Canonical process.

The Finding and Publication of the Scrolls[1]

In 1947, a merchant from Bethlehem came into possession of seven scrolls that had been recently uncovered in a cave in the Judean wilderness. This merchant, reportedly nicknamed Kando, came to possess them by local bedouin who had recently stumbled across a cave filled with jars and ancient manuscripts.[2] While the bedouin did not know what they were dealing with precisely, they sensed potential value in the scrolls because, clearly, they were very old. Ironically, however, while Kando had dealings in antiquities, he didn't fully understand the value of this transaction either. As we

---

1. For very useful surveys on the finding of the scrolls, see Jodi Magness, *The Archaeology of Qumran and the Dead Sea Scrolls* (Grand Rapids: William B. Eerdmans, 2002); James VanderKam, *The Dead Sea Scrolls Today* (Grand Rapids: William B. Eerdmans, 1994).

2. Magness, *Qumran and the Dead Sea Scrolls*, 26.

will see in just a moment, his price for the scrolls was nothing compared to the selling price of the scrolls later down the line.

Over the next few months, inquiries were put out regarding potential buyers. Word eventually reached a Syrian Orthodox Archbishop named Athanasius Samuel, who purchased four scrolls for $100. Those scrolls included what came to be identified as a complete copy of the scroll of Isaiah, a commentary on the book of Habakkuk, the so-called Community Rule, and the Genesis Apocryphan. By 1948, Samuel had contacted John Trever at the American Schools of Oriental Research in order to confirm the authenticity of the four scrolls, photograph them, and see what could be done about an initial publication. Eventually Samuel made his way to America where he sold them to Yigael Yadin, who in 1954 purchased the four scrolls for the nation of Israel for around $250,000. This price translates to a 2,500% return on Samuel's investment!

Roughly concurrently to Samuel, Eleazar Sukenik of the Hebrew University had also come into possession of some scrolls: a less complete scroll of Isaiah, the War Scroll, and the Hymn Scroll. Being trained in issues of ancient manuscripts, he immediately recognized their authenticity and value, Consequently, he sought to procure as many scrolls as he could.

The initial seven scrolls of the Dead Sea corpus came from a cave in the immediate proximity of a site called Khirbet Qumran. And once the contents of those scrolls were initially published, and people began to understand the value of these scrolls, bedouins and scholars alike sought out more caves in the area. Yet efforts to find more scrolls were interrupted with the concluding events of World War II. And when the dust settled, the region was allotted to Jordan, who quickly sanctioned the first systematic excavations of that original cave. Led by Roland de Vaux and G. Lankester Harding, excavations focused upon the cave and the nearby settlement of Qumran. Interesting, de Vaux and Harding initially failed to make a connection between the cave the nearby site. As we shall see, the nature of this relationship is accepted by many but is still debated.

Khirbet Qumran sits in the immediate vicinity of the Dead Sea, which is approximately 400 meters below sea level. There is no usable water source close to Qumran, and the nearby springs are unusable do to their salinity levels. Consequently, given the topographical and ecological characteristics of the region, it comes as no surprise that prior to the discovery of the Dead Sea Scrolls Qumran enjoyed very little visitation by geographers and archaeologists. It was only a site about which many geographers and schol-ars made passing comments.

One of the first to visit was Louis-Féicien Caignart de Saulcy around 1850. He noted the presence of the ruins and appeared to identify the site as biblical Gomorrah. However, Saulcy's notes were confusing, and Henry B. Tristram was unable to verify his identification of Qumran as biblical Gomorrah. Later, in 1874, Charles Clermont-Ganneau excavated a cave near Qumran as well as some nearby graves. He found nothing of value in the caves, but he did describe that the graves were neither Christian nor Muslim. Clermont-Ganneau also rejected the identification of Qumran as Gomorrah. Finally, in 1914 Gustaf Dalman noted the remnants of walls at the site and eventually classified it as a "fort," a classification that remained widely influential until the discovery of the scrolls in the 1940s.

In 1951 de Vaux and Harding finally made the connection between the caves surrounding Qumran and the site of Qumran. By analyzing the pottery found in the caves and at the site (jar handles, cooking pots, oil lamps, etc.), the excavators determined that the people who inhabited Qumran were those that used the caves most likely for storage.[3] But this was not the only important conclusion made by de Vaux and Harding at this point. They also articulated the Essence hypothesis, an idea about the identification of the Qumran community that has proven to be widely influential but has recently been subjected to criticism (see below). In ad-dition, de Vaux and Harding determined that Qumran was not a Roman site, a conclusion linked to a conviction that the stone used to construct the site was not of Roman quality. They also determined two or three distinct phases of occupation, the final phase of which ended with a massive fire. Yet most interestingly, de Vaux and Harding were ahead of their time by several decades when they made use of Carbon-14 dating techniques to verify elements of their chronological reconstruction.

As de Vaux and Harding were conducting their excavations, the local bedouin continued to look for more caves. This meant that de Vaux and Harding were continually pulled away from Qumran to verify new finds and new caves. Caves 2–4 were found in the early 1950s, and by 1956, 11 caves had been found. Caves 1, 2, 4, 6, and 11 were found by the bedouin, and caves 3, 5, and 7–10 were discovered by archaeologists.[4]

---

3. Magness, *Qumran and the Dead Sea Scrolls*, 27.

4. Magness, *Qumran and the Dead Sea Scrolls*, 29.

Cumulatively, about 900 different manuscripts with thousands of manuscript fragments were found, which doesn't consider the 30 caves that were also found farther to the north and south of Qumran.[5] All of this produced a glut of manuscript evidence that saturated the market in the span of about 10 years. Of course, this is a doubled edged sword. On the one hand, a whole new world was there waiting to be unlocked and understood. On the other hand, processing such a huge corpus was a herculean task. The catalog needed to be analyzed and published. Thankfully, the scholarly community quickly realized the importance of such an endeavor. Yet as will be discussed below, efforts to analyze and publish the Dead Sea Scrolls were undermined by several issues. But before this story is revisited, it's important to discuss briefly some important features of Qumran the site.

Roland de Vaux articulated the occupational history of Qumran in three distinct phases. He argued that the first phase of notable occupation began in the second century BCE, around 130 BCE[6] and lasted until approximately 100 BCE. A second phase, which saw the implementation of

5. According to the pottery assemblages of these caves, they too have been associated with the Qumran community.

6. de Vaux had difficult determining a starting point for the site. The site showed evidence of Iron Age occupation (e.g. a *lmlk* jar handle and cisterns), but without coinage, which proved to be very important for dating the subsequent phases of occupation, de Vaux's reconstruction was hindered.

the architectural footprint that would serve the site until its destruction by the Romans ranged from 100–31 BCE.[7] At that time, Qumran experienced a devastating earthquake that may have been accompanied by a fire (the evidence is unclear). de Vaux dated this to 31 BCE by means of Josephus's testimony. After 31 BCE, de Vaux argued for a period of abandonment until approximately 4 BCE, when the same group rebuilt the site and ushered in the final phase of occupation. This phase lasted until 68 CE when the Romans destroyed the site in conjunction with the events of the Jewish War. Bracketing this span of notable occupation, 130ish BCE–68 CE, de Vaux suggested minimal Iron Age occupation and Roman occupation, that latter of which was most likely associated with Roman military presence in the region.

de Vaux's chronology is generally accepted, although it has encountered some criticism. For example, Magness argues that de Vaux's Phase 1a did not exist, and his dating of the genesis for the sectarian community at Qumran is pushed too far back. Instead, Magness says the sectarian community of Qumran was established sometime between 100–50 BCE and that the first phase of occupation should be subdivided by the earthquake of 31 BCE. Moreover, she rejects any notion of a lengthy period of abandonment after the earthquake.[8] In other words, Magness believes that Qumran was inhabited for a shorter period of time but more continuously.

Identifying the sectarian community of Qumran has been the subject of significant debate. The suggestion that the community at Qumran was an Essene community has been widely influential, but it suffers from a lack of explicit evidence.[9] At no place does the literature of Qumran mention the term Essene. Moreover, the Essene hypothesis hinges on the testimony of ancient authors, such as Josephus, Philo, and Pliny. And Pliny's description, which happens to be the best evidence for the Essene theory, is hampered by unclarity.[10] Nevertheless, the archaeological evidence, as well as the texts,

7. de Vaux's second phase, which be called Ib, was distinguished architecturally from the first, Ia. The architectural footprint phase Ib was highlighted by a large tower entrance as well as several kitchens, kiln rooms, and storage rooms. Together, the footprint of Ib suggests a site whose daily activities were diverse. Most importantly, such a footprint contrasts that of phase Ia and was not significantly altered during Phase II.

8. Magness, *Qumran and the Dead Sea Scrolls*, 67–69.

9. VanderKam offers a lengthy discussion of this hypothesis, including the pros and cons. VanderKam, *The Dead Sea Scrolls*, 70–97.

10. Wise, Abegg, and Cook argue against the Essene connection in the context of arguing against what they call the "Standard Model," which holds to an Essene connection,

suggest a community—Essene or not—that saw themselves as an apocalyptic group buying their time before the end of the age. The War Scroll makes this and other convictions clear. The members of this community believed they were the recipients of biblical prophecy and the faithful followers of the enigmatic Teacher of Righteousness.[11]

The community subjected themselves to a very strict, regimented lifestyle that was obsessed with achieving and maintaining purity. Associated with this commitment appears to have been Qumran's elaborate water system, which brought water approximately 750 yards into the settlement from the nearby Wadi Qumran. Many believe that this delivery system fed the ceremonial baths strategically positioned throughout the site. Ironically, however, de Vaux argued against the notion that Qumran was a site rich in strategically positioned ceremonial baths. But as Magness has argued, when the archaeological evidence is interpreted in tandem with the textual evidence, it seems clear that Qumran was a site obsessed with purity, and its water delivery system was at the heart of it. Thus, many historians and archaeologists point to this sophisticated water delivery system, which pooled flash floods and seasonal rains in a dammed pool, as the most impressive feature of the site.

Editing and Publishing the Dead Sea Scrolls

While preliminary publications of the Dead Sea Scrolls began in 1948, 1951 marked the publication of the first complete edition. Of the first seven scrolls found, the large Isaiah scroll and the commentary on Habakkuk were first to be published.[12] From there, publication was steady and relatively quick through the mid-1950s. By 1956, the original seven

an anti-Hasmonean sentiment among the members of the community, and a connection between Qumran and the nearby caves. Michael Wise, Martin Abegg, Jr., and Edward Cook, *The Dead Sea Scrolls: A New Translation* (New York: HarperCollins, 2005), 16–26. Also, VanderKam provides a substantive discussion on the problems with the Essene connection as well as alternative theories, which include a Sadducean group and a group from Jerusalem who were fleeing the Romans. VanderKam, *The Dead Sea Scrolls*, 87–97.

11. This assumes a connection between the site and the caves where the texts were found. However, this too has been called into question. For example, Wise, Abegg, and Cook site a study by Joseph Patrich and others that highlight the absence of any pathways from the site to the caves. See Wise, Abegg, and Cook, *The Dead Sea Scrolls*, 23–24.

12. Millar Burrows, *The Dead Sea Scrolls of St. Mark's Monastery; Volume I: The Isaiah Manuscript and the Habakkuk Commentary* (New Haven, CT: American Schools of Oriental Research, 1951).

scrolls had been published. However, according to VanderKam, problems started with Cave 4.[13]

This cave is the most famous of the 11 because the quantity of manuscripts found were simply overwhelming. Cave 4 produced thousands of fragments. Thus, it became clear that a team was needed to sift through the manuscripts and lead the publication efforts of the remaining scrolls and

13. James VanderKam, *The Dead Sea Scrolls Today*, 188.

scroll fragments. Eventually, a team of seven scholars was amassed to join de Vaux: Frank Moore Cross; J. T. Milik, John Allegro, Jean Starcky, Patrick Skehan, John Sturgnell, and Claus-Hunno Hunzinger.[14]

One of the first things that the committee commissioned was the construction of a concordance. This document would catalog not only the words that appeared in these fragments but also the location of their occurrences. By detailing what words appeared where, the members of the team could quickly cross-reference other locations of particular words. Despite this, publication efforts soon faced significant headwinds. First, the Rockefeller funds that had been underwriting publication efforts lapsed. Then the effects of the 6 Day war dictated that the region of the Dead Sea transfer ownership from the Jordanians to the Israelis. There was also the pace of publication. To say that it slowed would be an understatement. As VanderKam details, the years between publications increased and the ideology informing publication efforts shifted.[15]

Then there was the tension between members of the committee. VanderKam describes how John Allegro effectively went rogue, publishing several unsanctioned works that crossed the line into unsubstantiated and outlandish theories.[16] Finally, there was the turnover between members of the committee and a tightly watched restriction on the number of committee members. Only when a member passed away or decided to step down would a replacement be approved. Thus, the size of the committee was effectively locked at 8. The problem here was that a committee of this size was just not feasible vis-à-vis the hoard of manuscripts that needed to be processed and published.

14. VanderKam, *The Dead Sea Scrolls*, 189.

15. As noted by VanderKam, the editors become more concerned with exhaustiveness than speed VanderKam, *The Dead Sea Scrolls*, 190–91.

16. VanderKam, *The Dead Sea Scrolls*, 191.

Then in the 1980s several events forced a change in the status quo surrounding the project. First, there was a rise in conspiracies theories as vocal members of the scholarly community at large became increasingly frustrated with the pace of publication. Hershel Shanks is probably the most famous case. Shanks was the founder and editor of *Biblical Archaeology Review*, and he used his publications to ratchet up the rhetoric and negative sentiments around the committee's efforts. Also, Robert Eisenman and Philip Davies reportedly attempted to gain access to some unpublished scrolls. Second, publication efforts cross-pollinated with politics. In 1990, the Israeli Antiquities Authority appointed Emanuel Tov to be co-director of the project, much to the chagrin of John Sturgnell. Sturgnell then gave an interesting interview wherein he made some disparaging comments about Judaism, all of which apparently helped lead to his firing. In his place, Tov, Emile Puech, and Eugene Ulrich all became co-directors of the project.

The final blows came in the early 1990s. On one front, the Huntington Library in San Marino, CA published their photographs of the Dead Sea Scrolls in 1991.[17] Apparently, these photographs were the gift of Eliza-

17. See John Noble Wilford, "Monopoly Over Dead Sea Scrolls is Ended," *New York Times*, Sept. 22, 1991, https://www.nytimes.com/1991/09/22/us/monopoly-over-dead-sea-scrolls-is-ended.html (accessed on Jan 8, 2019).

beth Bechtel, a well-known supporter of the project.[18] Similarly, Hershel Shanks and *Biblical Archaeology Review* published over 1700 photographs in their two-volume *A Facsimile Edition of the Dead Sea Scrolls*.[19] Yet the most ingenuous move came from two people at Hebrew Union College in Cincinnati, OH. As mentioned, the project published concordances of words that were used throughout the Dead Sea corpus. A particular characteristic of these concordances was that they also gave the words in the immediate context of the term in focus. So, if one could gain access to these concordances, in theory one could possibly reconstruct not only lines but entire manuscripts and scrolls. One just needed time, a proper method, and adequate processing power. Martin Abegg and Ben Zion Wacholden of Hebrew Union College tackled the theory and ran these concordances through computer programs to reconstruct the texts.[20] Sure enough, in 1991, the Hebrew Union College edition was published: *A Preliminary Edition of the Unpublished Dead Sea Scrolls*.[21] Thus, the hand of the committee was forced.

The Implications of the Dead Sea Scrolls

Similar to Ugarit, the importance of the Dead Sea Scrolls for the Old Testament rises and falls with its texts. On the one hand, they illuminated the vast thought-world of early Judaism. The texts showed a wide variety of perceptions toward the central power structures and social institutions of the time, as well as a variety of theologies. And there have been some who have been quick to connect the ideology of the Qumran community with the ideology of the early Church, suggesting a possible relationship.[22] However, VanderKam is correct when he encouraged a more

18. VanderKam, *The Dead Sea Scrolls*, 195. According to Wilford's article, Huntington's acquisition of the photographs began when Bechtell fell out with James A. Sanders at the Ancient Biblical Manuscript Center in Claremont, CA.

19. Robert H. Eisenman and James M. Robinson, eds., *A Facsimile Edition of the Dead Sea Scrolls* (2 vols.; Washington, D. C.: Biblical Archaeology Society, 1991).

20. For their account of the process, see Wise, Abegg, and Cook, *The Dead Sea Scrolls*, 7–8.

21. Martin G. Abegg and Ben Zion Wacholder, eds., *A Preliminary Edition of the Unpublished Dead Sea Scrolls* (Washington, D. C.: Biblical Archaeology Society, 1991).

22. In a lengthy discussion, VanderKam points to similarities in between the practices, eschatological perceptions and convictions, and literature. VanderKam, *The Dead Sea Scrolls*, 162–84.

critical posture. Indeed, there are similarities, but they are not indicative of any genetic relationship. Rather, "The Qumran literature has shown to a far greater extent than what was sensed before 1947 how deeply rooted early Christianity was in the Jewish soil that nourished it."[23] Qumran, therefore, shows the culminations of the ideological and theological trajectories that were still developing in the years when the books of the Old Testament were being finalized.

But without a doubt, when it comes to Qumran's most enduring significance for Old Testament studies, it's about textual criticism and the Canonical process. Simply, the texts of Qumran offer a window into the Canonization process and the discipline of textual criticism that just did not exist before 1947. Consider this. At Qumran, an edition of Jeremiah was found that was not only significantly shorter than the text of Jeremiah found in our English translations, but also is organized differently.[24] Similarly, there are major variations in certain Psalms, the book of Daniel, and Samuel. So, given that this site was active during Jesus's day, the first century CE, one must concede that textual standardization was not a reality. Moreover, Tov has succinctly, but accurately, described a "plurality" of texts that were in existence during the first century.[25] The diverse manuscripts that existed at Qumran demonstrates this, and naturally, this moves Qumran to the forefront for establishing the dynamics and history of the manuscript traditions.

What makes Qumran so fascinating is that one could go in any number of directions when trying to tease out the textual critical implications of Qumran's manuscripts. For example, it would be possible to invoke the evidence of Qumran to discuss the distinct methods and families of textual preservation. According to Tov there are five observable categories,[26] all of which is incredibly complicated, layered, and nuanced. Yet instead of creating a fog of confusion, and at the chance of sounding glib, I want to discuss Qumran's implications for textual criticism and the Canonical process.

23. VanderKam, *The Dead Sea Scrolls*, 184.

24. VanderKam, *The Dead Sea Scrolls*, 128–30.

25. Emanuel Tov, *Textual Criticism of the Hebrew Bible* (sec. and rev. ed.; Minneapolis: Fortress Press, 2001), 155–97. For the "local texts theory," see Frank Moore Cross, "The Evolution of a Theory of Local Texts" in *Qumran and the History of the Biblical Text* (eds. Frank Moore Cross and Shemaryahu Talmon; Cambridge: Harvard University Press, 1976), 306–20. Cross argued that certain textual traditions evolved because of geographic considerations.

26. Tov, *Textual Criticism*, 114–17.

And I want to do this by painting the briefest of pictures. By envisioning the development of the Old Testament text through broad contours, I will eventually show how the Qumran texts fit into the picture of the Old Testament's development and process of textual criticism.

The books of the Old Testament are the result of a complicated process that brought together individual texts and traditions because of their authoritative qualities. Put simply, they were deemed by Israel to communicate important elements about God's revelation. At some point, adjustments to the texts ceased and each reached a final form.[27] However, this does not mean that the text was free from any further alteration. Deviations from that final form crept in due to several factors during the copying process, including human error, intentional alteration (for clarification, explanation, or methodological preference), and the implications of geographically separated communities. Remember, there was no printing press, and everything was done by hand. Inevitably, and frustratingly, those deviations were preserved and/or further developed by subsequent copying processes, to the point that one may be inclined to speak about "multiple forms of a book" (see above).

Consequently, one can see the trajectory. A proliferation of texts. That is, a plurality of texts, and this brings us back to Qumran. There, existing in the same geographic location—side by side—were individual manifestations of this textual plurality. In other words, Qumran offers a historically anchored, cross-section of the complex process of textual transmission and Canonization. But it goes further than this. The youngest texts at Qumran actually represent the twilight of this textual plurality, for late in the first century CE there was a movement afoot to standardize these texts. Consequently, any variation observed in Dead Sea Scrolls can potentially be an important voice in the search for an original reading, a reading that reflects the moment when a book reached its final form. The chart below visualizes what has just been described.

27. This assumes a specific posture about authorship and the development of texts in antiquity that is foreign to many modern Christians. The notion of "authorship" and "literary production" did not operate with the same canons and expectations as modern literary production. See Schniedewind's *How the Bible Became a Book* as well as Karel van der Toorn, *Scribal Culture and the Making of the Hebrew Bible* (Cambridge: Harvard University Press, 2007) and John Walton and Brent Sandy, *The Lost World of Scripture: Ancient Literary Culture and Biblical Authority* (Downers Grove, IL: IVP Academic, 2013) for useful discussions.

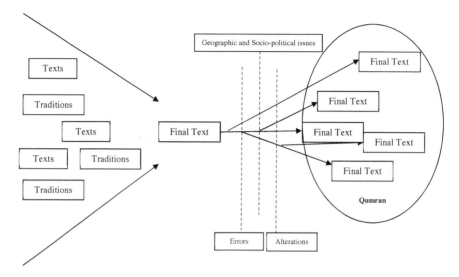

If there is one sub-discipline within Old Testament studies that is thoroughly complex, it's textual criticism and its relationship to the Canonical process. And in some ways, Qumran only adds to the confusion. Nevertheless, the discoveries at Qumran are indispensable for they testify how ancient communities preserved and perpetuated their authoritative texts through time.

Narrow Convergences

6

The Tel Dan Stele

W hen excavating, archaeologists and their teams look at everything. I mean *everything*. Why? Because you just don't know what you are going to find. Archaeologists don't just look at the dirt below their feet. They look at the dirt on the walls of the balks. They take buckets of excavated dirt to the sifter in the outside chance that something critically important was missed. For example, scarabs, coins, weights, jewelry, and other valuable small finds are often found in the sifter. Yet despite the excitement of potentially finding something of value in the least likely of places, you don't want to be the person tagged for sifting duty.

Sifting entails taking buckets of dirt and filtering them one-by-one through a waist-high frame of metal messing. As you shake the frame violently, chunks of dirt break apart and dust falls into buckets (or a pile) at your feet leaving any worthwhile object, such as a scarab, seal, coin, or an inscriptional fragment, on top of the meshing. Unfortunately, after about 30 minutes of this—dirt flying and wind blowing—you look like someone who has just wandered in from the desert having survived a sandstorm. You look barely human, and you will be digging dirt out of your nose for the next week.

But again, the reason archaeologists sift is because material was discarded and reused every day, and some of that material produces some of the most excited finds. Perhaps the famous example of discarded material changing the landscape of Old Testament studies happened at Tel Dan.

The Tel Dan Fragments

In the summer of 1993, the excavators of Tel Dan were focusing on an area located near the outer gate of the city, and the stratum under examination was dated to the middle of Iron Age II. At some point a volunteer noticed a peculiar looking stone sticking out of a wall constructed for a courtyard, which was about 400 square meters.[1] The stone was of a "high quality," and upon further examination writing was observed. In turn, the excavators excavated it, eventually giving it the name Fragment A. The next season, two other small fragments were discovered. Fragment B1 was discovered in a pile of debris about two meters south of a standing stone construction,[2]

1. Avraham Biran and Joseph Naveh, "An Aramaic Stele Fragment from Tel Dan," *IEJ* 43.2–3 (1993): 81.

2. Avraham Biran and Joseph Naveh, "The Tel Dan Inscription: A New Fragment," *IEJ* 45.1 (1995): 2.

and Fragment B2 was identified among paving stones about eight meters north of Fragment B1.[3]

All three fragments were of local basalt and appeared to have come from the same stone prepared for inscribing. An iron stylus was probably used.[4]

Frag. A measures 32 cm x 22 cm (at its maximum width) and contains 13 lines.[5] Frag. B1 measures 20 cm x 1.4 cm thick, but the writing surface is approximately 15 cm x 11 cm and contains six lines of text.[6] Fragment B2 is 10 cm x 9 cm but exhibits 4 lines of text on a 9 cm x 6 cm surface.[7] Biran and Naveh speculate that the dimensions of the original inscription were approximately 1m x 50cm.[8]

The language is undoubtedly Old Aramaic. Other than the letters that have been disturbed from the destruction, the script is remarkably clear. The text is dated paleographically, that is by the style of writing, from the middle to the latter part of the ninth century. However, Biran and Naveh admitted that this dating should not be taken definitively. "It might fall within a range of some decades earlier or later."[9] Baruch Halpern concurred when he stated that the epigraphy "is part neither of the 10th/9th century nor the 8th/7th Aramaic epigraphic tradition, but it is on the cusp of each."[10] Hagelia agrees that precise dating via paleography is elusive, but admits that a paleographic analysis is an important contribution.[11]

Dating the inscription's time of composition and destruction by means of stratigraphic analysis is difficult. As already mentioned, each fragment was found in secondary usage. Moreover, a destruction level, identified with the Neo-Assyrian king Tiglath-Pilesar III (ca. 730 BCE), covered each fragment.[12] However, the latest pottery shards of the as-

---

3. Biran and Naveh, "A New Fragment," 5.

4. Biran and Naveh, "An Aramaic Stele Fragment," 84-86.

5. Biran and Naveh, "An Aramaic Stele Fragment," 84.

6. Biran and Naveh, "A New Fragment," 2

7. Biran and Naveh, "A New Fragment," 5.

8. Biran and Naveh, "An Aramaic Stele Fragment," 84.

9. Biran and Naveh, "An Aramaic Stele Fragment," 95.

10. Baruch Halpern, "The Stela from Dan: Epigraphic and Historical Consider-ations," *BASOR* 296 (1994): 68.

11. Hallvard Hagelia, *The Dan Debate: The Tel Dan Inscription in Recent Research* (Recent Research in Biblical Studies 4; Sheffield: Sheffield Phoenix Press, 2009), 130–31. Hagelia's volume is an indispensable resource in articulating the contours of this debate.

12. Biran and Naveh, "An Aramaic Stele Fragment," 85-86; Biran and Naveh, "A New

semblage beneath the pavement date to the end of the ninth/beginning of the eighth centuries.[13] Consequently, the inscription was destroyed and reused around the beginning of the eighth century. Anything more precise is just too problematic.

Furthering the difficulties of the inscription, the line that would have declared the author is lost. In 1993, Biran and Naveh proposed that the author of the stele was a vassal king to the king of Aram-Damascus, and that Ahab was responsible for its destruction.[14] Baruch Halpern suggested that Ben-Hadad II was responsible for its composition. Subsequently, either Joash or Jeroboam II restored Israelite control to the region and so destroyed the monument.[15] Upon finding the final two fragments, Biran and Naveh altered their initial opinion. They suggested that composition be dated during the time of Hazael, a contemporary of Jehu.[16] Interestingly, Biran and Naveh do not give a new suggestion of who might be responsible for its destruction.

In 1995, Biran and Naveh offered the first translation of the inscription. It read as follows.[17]

[. . .] and cut [. . .]

[. . .] my father went up [against him when] he fought at [. . .]

And my father lay down, he went to his [ancestors]

And the king of I[s—]

rael entered previously in my father's land. [And] Hadad made me king.

And Hadad went in front of me, [and] I departed from [the] seven [. . .]

s of my kingdom, and I slew [seve]nty kin[gs], who harnessed thou[sands of char—]

riots and thousands of horsemen (or: horses).
[I killed Jeho]ram son of [Ahab]

Fragment," 1-2,8.

13. Biran and Naveh, "A New Fragment," 8.

14. Biran and Naveh, "An Aramaic Stele Fragment," 96-98. This is based upon "my king" in line 6.

15. Halpern, "The Stela from Dan," 74.

16. Biran and Naveh, "A New Fragment," 17.

17. Biran and Naveh, "A New Fragment," 13.

king of Israel, and [I] killed [Ahaz]iahu son of [Jehoram kin—]

g of the House of David. And I set [there towns into ruins and turned]

their land into [desolation . . .]

other [. . .   and Jehu ru—]

led over Is[rael . . .   and I laid]

siege upon [. . .]

Response to the Find

The excitement surrounding this find is not hard to explain. Any time one of the greatest figures in the Old Testament is mentioned outside Scripture, people get excited. However, what makes the Tel Dan stele particularly fascinating is that the discovery of the fragments came at a time when some scholars were openly pondering the historical realities of Israel and David. P. R. Davies and T. L. Thompson published in 1992 influential monographs that questioned long held assumption about the history of Israel and the nature of Israelite culture during this period.[18] With the finding of these fragments,

18. P. R. Davies, *In Search of "Ancient Israel"* (JSOT Supp 148; Sheffield: JSOT Press, 1992); T. L. Thompson, *Early History of the Israelite People* (SHANE 4; Leiden: Brill,

a "tonic" against such claims was offered.[19] Nevertheless, as will be discussed now, strong opinions developed around this inscription, and the result was one of the liveliest debates in all Old Testament studies.

The authenticity of the inscription, the relationship of the fragments, the source of the inscription, and the consonants *bytdwd* will be discussed before a discussion of the stele's implications.[20]

The Authenticity of the Inscription

In 1994, Giovanni Garbini published an article online that questioned many of the initial conclusions about Fragment A.[21] Garbini focused on the initial dating and grammatical analysis put forth by Biran and Naveh. Moreover, he also compared the Tel Dan Stele with other well-known stele of the era. According to Garbini, oddity piles on oddity, resulting in the suggestion of forgery. Garbini also went on to suggest that the forger did his best to imitate the linguistic and orthographic phenomena of the Zakkur inscription, another Aramaic inscription of the ninth century.[22]

Yet Garbini was not an isolated voice of skepticism. That same year Frederick Cryer published his analysis of Fragment A.[23] He questioned the details and context of the find, the internal vowels, and the lack of a word divider between the consonants *byt* and *dwd*. Most provocatively, Cryer questioned the timing of the find—at a moment when question over the historicity of David and the biblical witness were as intense as they ever had been.

1992).

19. Halpern, "The Stela from Dan," 63.

20. I must restrict my discussion to these issues. Anything more is just too cumbersome for the purposes of this project. However, Hagelia has offered an important and exhaustive summary of the debate. See note 11.

21. Giovonni Garbini, "L'iscrizione aramaica di Tel Dan," *Atti della Academia nazionale dei Lincei, Scienze morali, storiche e filologiche, rendiconti* 9.5.3 (1994): 461–71. Hagelia references the English translation as an online publication, but at the time of this project the URL no longer functioned. Thus, this summary leans upon Hagelia, *The Dan Debate*, 13–18.

22. "The Inscription of Zakur: King of Hamath," translated by Alan Millard, (*COS*, 2.35).

23. Frederick H. Cryer, "On the Recently Discovered 'House of David' Inscription," *SJOT* 8 (1994): 3–20.

Another dissenting voice came in 2002, when Russel Gmirkin inter-estingly argued that the inscription was inscribed onto the stone *after* the stele was shattered.[24] Gmirkin asserts that traces of the letter can be dis-cerned on the edges of the inscription, a phenomenon that should not have been possible if the inscription was inscribed before it was shattered. How-ever, Hagelia has questioned the validity of such claims. "Gmirkin's photo-graphs are so bad that they cannot be considered to document anything."[25] Moreover, Hagelia questions the logic of Gmirkin's argument, creating the impression that Gmirkin may have manufactured his argument.

Hagelia's criticism of Gmirkin, while legitimate, does seem heavy handed. However, Hagelia's criticism was nothing compared to the inten-sity of the debate at the 1997 Biblical Archaeological Review Symposium featured on the cover of the July/August cover of *Biblical Archaeological Review*.[26] There, William Dever, Neils Peter Lemche, P. Kyle McCarter, and Thomas Thompson debated several issues related to the Tel Dan Stele, in-cluding its authenticity. At one point, Lemche went so far as to declare that the photographs published by the *Israel Exploration Journal* in the *editio princeps* were fakes. Such a claim incurred the annoyance and chastisement of Dever, who in turn defended the integrity of the excavation.

Truthfully, inscriptions are forged. Therefore, an inquiry into the le-gitimacy of any inscription should not be dismissed out of hand. However, any evidence that the Tel Dan Stele is a forgery is severely lacking. Most im-portantly, there are detailed accounts of the findings, including the details of its archaeological context. Such detail is the first indication of authentici-ty. Also, the purported grammatical "peculiarities," which were highlighted by skeptics of the inscription, are to be expected in such an inscription. One should not expect epigraphic Aramaic to exhibit the same features as later, more standardized manifestations of Aramaic.[27] Thus, any observed peculiarity may not be peculiar at all, rather indicative of the grammatical

---

24. Russel Gmirkin, "Tool Slippage and the Tel Dan Inscription," *SJOT* 16 (2002): 293–302.

25. Hagelia, *The Dan Debate*, 21.

26. Hershel Shanks, ed., "Biblical Minimalists Meet their Challengers Face to Face," *BAR* 23.4 (1997): 26–42; 66.

27. On analogy, Epigraphic Hebrew, or Hebrew derived solely from extrabiblical inscriptions, represents an earlier stage in the development of Hebrew and is thus less grammatically consistent. Sandra L. Gogel, *A Grammar of Epigraphic Hebrew* (SBL Re-sources for Biblical Studies 23; Atlanta: The Society of Biblical Literature, 1998).

features functioning at that moment. As Hagelia has said, emphasis upon the grammatical peculiarities "are precarious" and "unpersuasive."[28]

Relationship of the Fragments

Currently, the Tel Dan Stele is the sum of three inscriptional fragments, each of which were found in different locations and in secondary usage. This reality demands investigation into their relationship. Biran and Naveh in the *editio princeps* argued that they all should be joined. This, of course, produced several responses, and each of them can fall into one of three general categories.

- There are those who essentially agree with Biran and Naveh.

- There are those who agree that all three fragments came from the same inscription, but they disagree about the placement and proximity.

- There are those who argue that not all three fragments came from the same inscription.

The opinions that fall into the final category are the most radical. Moreover, one cannot help but notice the continuity between members of this third group with those are argue against the inscription's authenticity. Nevertheless, arguments for the separation of fragments all emphasize to one degree or another the inscription's epigraphic discontinuity. That is, they point to an apparent difference in writing style and a general lack of alignment between the lines. For example, Cryer and Thompson pointed to the discontinuity among the size of the letters as well as the varying space between the lines.[29] Bob Becking was more specific, but still leaned heavily upon apparent epigraphic variations. According to Becking, the spacing between letters in Fragment A was approximately seven percent wider than in Fragments B_1 and B_2.[30]

Details matter. So, Thompson, Cryer, Becking, and others are correct to stress the epigraphic details. However, as Hagelia stressed, irregularities

28. Hagelia, *The Dan Debate*, 17.

29. Frederick H. Cryer, "King Hadad," *SJOT* 9 (1995): 223–35; Thomas Thompson, "Dissonance and Disconnections: Notes on the Bytdwd and Hmlk.Hdd Fragments from Tel Dan," *SJOT* 9 (1995): 236–240.

30. Bob Becking, "The Second Danite Inscription Some Remarks," *BN* 81 (1996): 21-30.

on inscriptions are to be expected.[31] Thus, any assessment like those utilized by Thompson and company really comes down to establishing an ac-
ceptable level of stylistic irregularity. Put another way, at what point does
inconsistency become indicative of a different text? In the end, I echo Kott-
spierer and Detriech in the sense that arguments such as those by Becking,
Cryer, and company are difficult to accept.[32]

The debate around how exactly to position the three fragments has been
tamer. Essentially, scholars either agree with Biran and Naveh or not. Many
do agree with Biran and Naveh, and something of a consensus has formed.
However, there are a few dissenting voices. One of the most prominent is
Gershon Galil, who systematically argued that Fragments B1 and B2 come
well before Fragment A.[33] Similarly, George Athas agrees that Fragments A
was significantly separated from B1, and B2 in the original inscription, although he believes Fragment A came first (opposite of Galil).[34]

All things considered, it is wise to side with the spirit of Biran and
Naveh's reconstruction. Their reconstruction is certainly not unreasonable,
and the irregularities emphasized by their detractors are not overwhelming. All three fragments likely came from the same inscription and could
very well be placed in close proximity to each other. Moreover, if Hagelia
is right in pointing to the high-resolution photograph on the September
2001 cover of *Near Eastern Archaeology*, the debate on this issue may be
effectively closed.[35] Nevertheless, scholars will still do well to accept the

---

31. Hagelia, *The Dan Debate*, 27.

32. Walter Dietrich, "*dawid, dod*, und *bytdwd*," *TZ* 53 (1997): 30; Ingo Kottsieper,
"Die Inschrift vom Tell Dan und die politischen Beziehungen zwischen Aram-Damaskus
und Israel in der 1. Hälfte des 1. Jahrtausends vor Christus," in "*Und Mose schrieb dieses
Lied auf*": *Studien zum Alten Testament und zum Alten Orient. Festschrift für Oswald Loretz zur Vollendung seines 70. Lebensjahres mit Beiträgen von Freunden, Schülern un Kollegen. Unter Mitwirkung von Hanspeter Schaudig* (AOAT 250: Münster: Ugarit-Verlag,
1998), 476, n 4.

33. Gershon Galil, "A Re-arrangement of the Fragments of the Tel Dan Inscription
and the Relations between Israel and Aram," *PEQ* 133 (2001): 16–21.

34. George Athas, *The Tel Dan Inscription: A Reappraisal and a New Interpretation*
(JSOT Supp 360/CIS 12; Sheffield: Sheffield Academic Press, 2003), 189–91. More specifically, "Fragment B placed approximately 32 cm below Fragment A" (p. 191).

35. Hagelia references the photographs throughout chapter 4 (*The Dan Debate*,
22–31). In particular, "A new photograph seems to document a common fracture surface
between fragments A and B1 *beneath* the smooth top surface" (p. 22; emphasis mine).
Unfortunately, the common fracture surface is shaded by a shadow. Until further examination can be carried out, such a conclusion must remain tentative.

tentativeness of any reconstruction. William Schniedewind's 1996 statement is still appropriate. There is "room for new suggestions."[36]

Source of the Original Inscription

The debate about who sanctioned the inscription is robust, perhaps second only to the debate about the meaning and significance of the consonants *bytdwd*. Why? There is no explicit statement of origin among the fragments that have been discovered to date. Yet the debate is framed by a few general historical considerations. Based on the context of the finds, even though none of them were in a context of original usage, as well as an analysis of the writing style, the inscription was likely manufactured during the ninth century BCE.[37]

Assuming this framework, there are a few options. Unfortunately, all of them are complicated. First, Ben Hadad I. According to 1 Kgs 15:20, Ben Hadad reneged on his treaty with King Basha of Israel when King Asa of Judah swayed him with silver and gold. However, the problem with Ben Hadad I is that the proponents of this view based their conclusions by means of consulting only Fragment A.[38] Moreover, notable proponents of Ben Hadad I swayed their opinion upon the consultation of all three fragments, including the excavators.[39]

A second option is another Aramean king named Ben Hadad, to whom many people refer as Ben Hadad II. However, the historical identification of a Ben Hadad II is elusive. For example, the book of Kings refers to an Aramean king as a contemporary and nemesis of Ahab, which would situate the manufacturing of the stele firmly in the middle of the ninth century BCE. Yet only the moniker "Ben Hadad" is used (1 Kgs 10 and 22). Moreover, according to the Kurkh Monolith, the Aramean king Adad-idri

36. William M. Schniedewind, "Tel Dan Stela: New Light on Aramaic and Jehu's Revolt" *BASOR* 302 (1996): 77.

37. One of the B fragments was found in secondary usage as a paving stone, and this was immediately above a pottery assemblage that was dated to the eighth/ninth century transition. So, if the stele was destroyed and used as paving stones in the early part of the eighth century, say appr. 775 BCE, one should still look back to the ninth century, when the Aramean influence in the region was most intense, for its context of composition.

38. Hagelia, *The Dan Debate*, 32–33.

39. Compare Biran and Naveh, "An Aramaic Stele Fragment," 95 with Biran and Naveh, "A New Fragment," 17. Also, E. Lupinski, *The Arameans: Their Ancient History, Culture, Religion* (OLA 100; Leuven: Peeters, 2000), 376–78.

was a contemporary of Ahab and this name does not comport linguistically with Kings' Ben Hadad.[40] It is possible that Ben Hadad is some type of generic institutional or dynastic title, but as Lawson Younger, Jr. has stated, it does not alleviate all the problems.[41]

Without a doubt, Hazael is the most popular possibility. Hazael ruled in Damascus from the middle of the ninth century until the very end of that century.[42] During this period, Hazael was initially subdued by the Assyrians when Shalmaneser III asserted control over the region shortly after he came to the throne. Yet as Assyrian influence in the region waned, Hazael took the initiative to assert Aramean influence, expanding his sphere of influence southward into northern Israel.[43] Second Kings attests to this and contextualizes it in the reign of the Jehu dynasty (cf. 2 Kgs 10:32–33; 12:17–18; 13:22). The problem with the identification of Hazael as the source is that he was "a son of nobody," according to Assyrian sources. This phrase often denotes a usurper.[44] Thus, the reference to "my father" in the inscription creates an awkward dynamic.[45]

Hazael's son is also another option, and if things were not complicated enough, he is also called Ben Hadad in Kings (2 Kgs 13:3, 24–25)! Mentioned in the Zakkur Inscription, he reigned from about 803–775 BCE, but not many scholars have associated this third Ben-Hadad as the force behind the Tel Dan Stele.[46] Nevertheless, the most interesting theory about the inscription's origin was offered by Jan-Wim Wesselius, who ironically proposed that King Jehu of Israel was the benefactor of the inscription.[47]

40. Kyle Lawson Younger, Jr., "Aram and the Arameans," in *The World around the Old Testament* (eds. Bill T. Arnold and Brent A. Strawn; Grand Rapids: Baker Academic, 2016), 248–49.

41. While "Ben Hadad" is used in some contexts in a manner that supports the idea of a generic dynastic title (cf. 1 Kgs 15 vs. 1 Kgs 20 and 22 vs. 2 Kgs 13), it lacks the necessary support from external sources (Lawson Younger, Jr. "Aram and the Arameans," 249.).

42. Approximately 845–42 until 803 BCE. Lawson Younger, Jr., "Aram and the Arameans," 249.

43. Lawson Younger, Jr., "Aram and the Arameans," 249–53.

44. Lawson Younger, Jr., "Aram and the Arameans," 251.

45. However, according to Lemaire, the awkwardness is not beyond explanation. Andre Lemaire, "The Tel Dan Stele as a Piece of Royal Historiography," *JSOT* 81 (1998): 6.

46. Athas, *The Tel Dan Inscription*, 265; Gershon Galil, "A Re-arrangement," 18. Also, see Hagelia, *The Dan Debate*, 36–37.

47. Jan-Wim Wesselius, "The First Royal Inscription from Ancient Israel: The Tel

According to Wesselius, the biblical claim that Jehu killed off the Omride dynasty cannot be dismissed out of hand. Even more, Wesselius asserts that it is methodologically preferable to first disprove the main witness before moving to more radical theories. Thus, Wesselius' argument is largely a rebuttal against suggestions that a Jehu-origin is dubious. First, Wesselius envisions the legitimacy of an Aramaic inscription by an Israelite if Jehu was either a vassal or a supporter of Hazael's coup. Second, because Jehu demonstrated an accepting posture early in his reign (2 Kgs 10:18), it is not beyond the realm of reason for Jehu to have initially praised Hadad for his ascension. Third, it is well within the characteristics of royal literature in the ancient Near East to declare divine support in committing regicide. Fourth, referring to an Aramean king as his "father" is expected in contexts where one party (i.e. Jehu) is subservient to the other (the Aramean King). Wesslesius was criticized by Becking, and then again by Athas.[48] However, in 2001, before Athas' criticisms, Wesselius went on record saying that he was even more convinced in the wake of Becking's response.[49]

In the end, it is difficult to accept Wesselius' ideas. While he rightly champions not dismissing the biblical account off hand, there are too many contingencies for this scenario to play out. Wesselius' ideas are possible, but just not probable. It is ultimately best to accept the fact that the evidence *as it exists* prevents any definitive conclusion. Hazael may be the best guess, but any determination is just not certain. Nevertheless, if it was Hazael who sanctioned the construction of the stele, this scenario raises an important historical question that puts the biblical witness front and center. Who put an end to the Omride dynasty?

The Consonants *bytdwd*

In their initial publication, the excavators discussed the consonants *bytdwd* in a very focused way, and this decision had tremendous consequences. By not entertaining other possibilities for the consonants they effectively set the course for the avalanche of publications that would

---

Dan Inscription Reconsidered," *SJOT* 13 (1999): 163–86.

48. Athas, *The Tel Dan Inscription*, 257; Bob Becking, "Did Jehu Write the Tel Dan Inscription?" *SJOT* 13 (1999): 187–201.

49. Jan-Wim Wesselius, "The Road to Jezreel: Primary History and the Tel Dan Inscription," *SJOT* 15 (2001): 83–103.

follow. Without a doubt, understanding these six consonants is the critical issue for the Tel Dan Stele.

The editors read the consonants *bytdwd* as a construction chain, reading "the House of David." However, the lack of a word divider vis-à-vis the presence of word dividers throughout the inscription loomed large. Is it significant that there is no word divider between *byt* and *dwd*?

Many scholars accepted the reading of the excavators, but several dissenting voices soon rose to the occasion. For example, in 1994 Knauf, de Pury, and Römer collaborated and maintained that the phrase "the House of David" was an awkward reading for a few reasons, including historical, geographical, and grammatical ones. Moreover, they maintained that the reconstruction of the noun "king" immediately preceding *bytdwd* created a new set of problems.[50] Lemche and Thompson wondered if *bytdwd* is analogous to the place name *bytel*, or "Bethel."[51] Davies argued that the reconstruction of "king" before *bytdwd* was questionable, as well as the analogy between the "the House of David" and "the House of Omri."[52] Ben Zvi noted a lack of epigraphic evidence that supported reading *bytdwd* as a construct chain.[53]

In 1994, Andre Lemaire published a series of articles on the Mesha Stele, also known as the Moabite Stone. Among other things, Lemaire reconstructed the same consonants, *bytdwd*, without a word divider.[54] Thus, Lemaire offered a precedent for reading the consonants *bytdwd* without a word divider as a construct chain, *byt dwd*. Anson Rainey also found support for the excavators' reading in other Aramaic texts.[55] But the definitive a statement on the lack of a word divider came from Gary Rensburg. Compiling a host of Aramaic inscriptions, Rensburg argued that there is no word divider in the Tel Dan Stele because it was not required by the

50. Ernst Axel Knauf, D. de Pury, and Thomas Römer, "*Baytdawid ou *Baytdod? Une relecture de la nouvelle inscription de Tel Dan," *BN* 72 (1994): 65–66.

51. Niels Lemche and T. L. Thompson, "Did Biran Kill David? The Bible in Light of Archaeology," *JSOT* 64 (1994): 9.

52. P. R. Davies, "'House of David' Built on Sand: The Sins of the Biblical Maximizers," *BAR* 20.4 (1994): 54–55.

53. Ehud Ben Zvi, "On the Reading 'bytdwd' in the Aramaic Stele from Tel Dan," *JSOT* 64 (1994): 25–32.

54. Andre Lemaire, "'House of David' Restored in the Moabite Inscription," *BAR* 20.3 (1994): 30–37.

55. Anson Rainey, "The 'House of David' and the House of the Deconstructionists," *BAR* 20.6 (1994): 47

Aramaic of the Iron Age. Rensburg also argued that the chain *byt*XXX was a widely accepted Aramaic convention during the period.[56]

In a peculiar show of support, Hershel Shanks highlighted a private collector of antiquities, Shlomo Moussaieff. Moussaieff reportedly owns an ostracon that memorialized temple gift receipts and reads the prepositional phrase *lbytyhwh*, "to the House of the Lord." This orthography provides another example of a construct chain being written without any division between words.[57]

Consequently, the lack of a word divider has proven to be explainable. Yet the debate doubled down its intensity when scholars tried to determine the meaning of the phrase "the House of David." Hagelia and Galil have promoted several categories that frame the debate.[58]

First, "the House of David" refers to a dynastic family of Judah. Indeed, there have been some who advocate the subtlest of distinctions between a dynastic name and a name for Judah,[59] but Hagelia is correct to suggest that such an opinion is a distinction without a difference—a dynastic name is inextricably linked to its kingdom.[60] Second, *bytdwd* could refer to a toponym, an opinion often held by those who are hesitant to read *bytdwd* as a construct chain. Yet the speculative nature of this proposal has been emphasized.[61] Third, some suggest that *bytdwd* may refer to the temple in Jerusalem. Such an argument, however, assumes that the consonants *dwd* in *bytdwd* do not refer to a proper name but rather the generic idea of "beloved," which in turn is taken to refer to Yahweh. Thus, "the House of the Beloved," refers to "the House of Yahweh."[62] This is highly questionable and without adequate evidence. Similarly, perhaps *dwd* refers to a specific

56. Gary A. Rensburg, "On the Writing bytdwd in the Aramaic Inscription from Tel Dan," *IEJ* 45 (1995): 22–25.

57. Hershel Shanks, "Three Shekels for the Lord: Ancient Inscription Records Gift to Solomon's Temple," *BAR* 23.6 (1997): 28–32.

58. Galil, "A Re-arrangement," 16; Hagelia, *The Dan Debate*, 51–67.

59. Dietrich, "*dawid, dod,* und *bytdwd*," 28

60. Hagelia, *The Dan Debate*, 52.

61. Alan Millard, "Absence of Word Divider Proves Nothing," *BAR* 20.6 (1994): 68–69; David Freedman and J. C. Geoghegan, "'House of David' is There!" *BAR* 21.1 (1995): 78–79; Nadav Na'aman, "Beth-David in the Aramaic Stele from Tel Dan," *BN* 79 (1995): 18; Schniedewind, "Tel Dan Stele," 80.

62. Neils Lemche, "Bemerkungen über einen Paradigmenwechsel aus Anlaß einer neuentdeckten Inschrift," in *Meilenstein Festgabe für Herbert Donner zum 16. February 1995* (eds. M. Weippert and S. Timm; Ägypten und Altes Testament 30; Wiesbaden: Otto Harrassowitz, 1995), 104.

deity?[63] Unfortunately, there is no evidence that speaks of a deity named "Beloved."[64] Finally, Ben Zvi suggested that *bytdwd* refers to an unnamed official of the Judean court, which according to Ben Zvi is the best way to make sense of the reconstructed *mlk* immediately to *bytdwd*.[65]

Observing the debate over the consonants *bytdwd* from a bird's eye view, it's easy to scoff at some of the proposals. Some of them initially strike the reader as manufactured arguments born out of a stubborn refusal to accept the obvious. However, by not entertaining several possibilities, the excavators encouraged the debate. Yet in the end, the debate around the consonants displays the beauty of academic discourse. Initial proposals were criticized as necessary, with alternative proposals presented and subsequently criticized. In the end, a consensus formed that is now used as a launching pad for subsequent discourse. The consonants *bytdwd* are to be read as a construct chain, "the House of David," which refers to a particular Judean dynasty during Iron II.

The Implications of the Tel Dan Stele

The debates about the Tel Dan Stele uniquely brought into focus the emotion and passion of Biblical Studies. Indeed, debates about the Old Testament's historical usefulness and accuracy had taken place prior to the discovery of the stele fragments, reaching back to the eighteenth century and beyond. Yet the dynamics and context of the Tel Dan debate were different.

First, there was the David factor. David is a giant figure in the Old Testament. According to the Old Testament, David was the founder of the United Monarchy, the recipient of a dynastic promise, and the person whose legacy was felt perpetually after his death. He is intimately associated with Israel's cultic traditions and the root of messianic ideology. Consequently, to have such a figure mentioned outside the context of the Bible ensured strong opinions and an overwhelming response.

Beyond this, the state of biblical scholarship during the early 90s offered the perfect crucible for an intense debate. It was a time when the historical usefulness of the Old Testament was being questioned with new fervor. As detailed by Dever, certain voices within the debate derived their

63. Knauf, de Pury, and Römer, "*Baytdawid ou *Baytdod?" 66–67.

64. For example, see Kenneth Kitchen, "A Possible Mention of David in the Late Tenth Century BCE, and Deity *Dod as Dead as the Dodo?" *JSOT* 76 (1997): 29–44.

65. Ben Zvi, "Reading 'bytdwd," 28.

ideological foundation from postmodernity's deconstructionism, suggesting that this debate brought to fruition intellectual trajectories rooted in the 1970s.[66] Moreover, characterizations, stereotypes, and the collision of egos accompanied this debate. A result was the construction of two camps, the minimalists and the maximalists, and everyone found themselves in one of the camps whether they liked or agreed with it or not.

The minimalists were those who saw little or no historical value in the Old Testament, and they viewed its content with extreme skepticism. The maximalists, on the other hand, viewed the Old Testament as a useful historical source. Yet as is often the case in such instances, very few scholars fit neatly in one of the camps. Opinions were nuanced, and positions were tentative. Nevertheless, if one chose to weigh in on the debate, they would find themselves being pigeonholed.

But all things considered, the most important implication of the Tel Dan Stele is how it encouraged future debates about the Old Testament's historical usefulness to take shape. Questions about the historical usefulness of the Old Testament are rarely answered with black and white statements, as if any archaeological find could definitively prove or disprove the Old Testament's historical veracity. The Tel Dan Stele encouraged questions about the Old Testament's historical value to be framed in a more nuanced manner. To demonstrate this, consider the most prominent historical question raised by the stele, "Who was responsible to the death of Omride line?"

Despite the fragmentary nature of the inscription, there is a consensus that the originator of the monument claimed the eradication of the Omride dynasty.[67] This claim puts the stele in opposition to the Old Testament, assuming that Jehu is not the originator of the inscription (contra Wesselius; see above). According to 2 Kgs 9–10, Jehu was the divinely appointed instrument of judgment leveled at the House of Omri. So, which witness is correct? Is it as simple as an either/or proposition? Or, is there something more nuanced going on?

In an attempt to answer such questions, one must first consider the literary nature of the Old Testament. The Old Testament is ancient literature, and, as such, the communicative endeavors of the text are inextricably

---

66. William G. Dever, *What Did the Biblical Writers Know & When Did They Know It? What Archaeology Can Tell Us about the Reality of Ancient Israel* (Grand Rapids: William B. Eerdmans, 2001), 23–28.

67. The name Jehoram, successor of Amaziah (2 Kgs 1:17) and final monarch of the Omride line, is reconstructed in line 7.

linked to literary conventions of the ancient Near East. So, one must under-stand the method of communication in order to understand the claims of the text. When it comes to understanding 1 and 2 Kings and the Tel Dan Stele, an understanding of ancient Near Eastern royal literature is para-mount, which unfortunately also introduces its own set of variables. Royal literature is braggadocios and exploits literary ambiguity in order to present the sponsor of the text in as best light as possible.[68] Thus, the interpreter must be aware of the semantic demands vis-à-vis the semantic possibilities and be aware of the larger socio-political landscape and claims. Recon-struction is possible, but it requires a critical eye and must be held loosely.

In the case of the Omride dynasty's end, the Old Testament and the stele confirm the reality that its end took place at the end of the ninth cen-tury BCE when tensions between the Israelites and the Arameans were high. It was a time of socio-political fluidity between the regional powers. There-fore, is it possible to see multiple mechanisms for bringing down one of the region's most influential powers? It is noteworthy that the claims of the stele are somewhat nebulous. The text simply reads, "I killed Jehoram, son of Ahab," and the very generic root קתל is used. Such a bland statement is per-fect for a literary endeavor that seeks to stretch semantics for the benefit of the benefactor. Moreover, the Old Testament does acknowledge that Hazael wounded Jehoram in battle (2 Kgs 8:28). Nevertheless, the stele's ambiguity contrasts with the specificity of the Old Testament's account, which vividly pictures Jehu pulling back the bow, letting the arrow fly, and watching it run Jehoram through mid-back (2 Kgs 9:24).

Adding to the complexity is 2 Kgs 9:14, which reads, "Thus Jehu, son of Jehoshaphat, son of Nimshi conspired against Joram."[69] Here the verb קשר appears in the third person masculine singular form of the Hithpael stem. This form is rare in the Old Testament, save for a couple occurrences in 2 Chr 24:25–26. Semantically, it's possible to understand the sense to be a benefactive or estimative/declarative sense.[70] Either Jehu conspired against Joram for his own sake, or he was in a state of conspiring against Joram. Regardless, there is some ambiguity inherent to the syntax that precludes any semantic precision. By implication, does the ambiguous

68. Baruch Halpern has coined the "Tiglath Pileser Principle" that succinctly de-fines the essence of royal propaganda. Baruch Halpern, *David's Secret Demons: Messiah, Murderer, Traitor, King* (Grand Rapids: William B. Eerdmans, 2001), 124–32.

69. Joram is a bi-form of Jehoram.

70. *IBHS*, 26.2e–f.

syntax allow one to consider the possibility of collusion between a newly sanctioned usurper and the traditional enemies of the Omride dynasty?[71] If so, is the collision of the Tel Dan Stele and 2 Kgs an example of converging historiographic perspectives?

Unfortunately, any definitive answer currently eludes interpreters. However, the notion of converging historiographic perspectives is an important issue to consider when interpreting the Old Testament. When there are multiple perspectives about a particular topic or event, how does the interpreter assess and wade through the possibilities? Does it become an exercise of jettisoning one at the expense of the other? Or, is a synthesis possible? These and other related questions loom large, and they will bubble to the surface again in the next chapter.

---

71. Biran and Naveh also ponder this when they wonder if Jehu was Hazael's agent. Biran and Naveh, "A New Fragment," 18.

7

The Taylor Prism

On the twelfth of Abu, 705 BCE, Sennacherib was crowned king of the mighty Neo-Assyrian Empire, when his father, Sargon II, died tragically in battle. Sennacherib had been groomed for such a moment, having already led several military campaigns for his father.[1] Over the next two and a half decades, Sennacherib would sanction over ten military campaigns and oversee massive building drives in several notable Assyrian cities, including Aššur, Nineveh, and Tarbiqu.[2] He is one of the most famous kings of the Neo-Assyrian Empire on the record, and his shadow across the Old Testament is arguably the greatest of any Neo-Assyrian king.

The Taylor Prism

The sources that document Sennacherib's reign are abundant and diverse. The genres range from historiographic texts, administrative letters, astrological records, to many more.[3] One important medium were the clay prisms. These octagonal or hexagonal shapes replaced the smaller clay cylinders, presumably because the prisms offered more surface area on which to write. According to Grayson and Novotny, the transition to clay prisms occurred around 698 BCE,[4] and most prisms date to the short period between 698–689 BCE,[5] with the majority of and most famous hexagonal

---

1. A. K. Grayson and Jamie Novotny, *The Royal Inscriptions of Sennacherib, King of Assyria (704–681 BE), Part 1* (Winona Lake, IN: Eisenbrauns, 2012), 1. Also, for a detailed summary of Sennacherib's time as crown prince, see Josette Elayi, *Sennacherib, King of Assyria* (Atlanta: SBL Press, 2018), 29–42.

2. Grayson and Novotny, *The Royal Inscriptions*, 1.

3. Grayson and Novotny, *The Royal Inscriptions*, 1

4. Grayson and Novotny, *The Royal Inscriptions*, 2

5. Grayson and Novotny, *The Royal Inscriptions*, 4

prisms dating between 691–689 BCE.[6] Upon completion, these prisms were deposited in several different contexts, including armories and other culturally significant sites.

The Taylor Prism is a hexagonal clay prism that is virtually identical to two other prisms: the Chicago Prism and the Jerusalem Prism. Together, they comprise a critical element to a significant body of literature labeled Sennacherib's Annals. According to Grayson and Novotny, the inscriptions on these prisms were produced between fourteenth and sixteenth regnal years of Sennacherib, and it may be possible to understand the Jerusalem Prism as the oldest of the lot, for its building account is shorter than the Taylor and Chicago Prisms respectively.[7] The Chicago and Jerusalem Prisms were deposited in the armory, near the citadel, along the western wall of Nebi-Yunis, one of the main mounds that comprised the ancient city of Nineveh. The Taylor Prism is named for Colonel J. Taylor, the British official who ultimately came into possession of the prism.

Exactly *how* Colonel Taylor came into possession of the prism is impossible to reconstruct. First, Austen Layard's statement that Colonel Taylor was in possession of the artefact is contradicted by King and Oppert.[8] Second, one can only guess if the prism was discovered at Nebi-Yunis along with the Chicago and Jerusalem Prisms. Some argue that the Taylor Prism was found at the Kuyunik mound, one of the other major mounds that

6. Grayson and Novotny, *The Royal Inscriptions*, 5

7. Grayson and Novotny, *The Royal Inscriptions*, 5

8. Sven Pallis, *The Antiquity of Iraq: A Handbook of Assyriology* (Copenhagen: Ejnar Munksgaard, 1956), 69

comprised ancient Nineveh.[9] Third, it is unclear *when* the British museum came into possession of the find. What's clear is that the British Museum had come into possession of the prism sometime before 1861, for this is the year when they published the prism's content. An updated reading was published in 1909.[10]

The Taylor Prism recounts, among other things, Sennacherib's third military campaign, which took place sometime during Sennacherib's third or fourth regnal years—701 BCE.[11] Generally, the campaign was in response to the widespread rebellion across his empire in the wake of Sargon II's untimely death. More specifically, it was a response to the overt rebellion by many of his vassals of the Levant, in which Hezekiah and Judah appear to have played an important role.[12] Yet Assyriologists often divide Sennacherib's third campaign into three phases largely based on geography.[13] First, the king swept down the Phoenician coast, targeting the king of Sidon. Sidon's king fled to Cyprus, and Sennacherib installed a pro-Assyrian king in his stead. Then, the Assyrian set his sights further south along to coast to hostile Philistine regions. Ashkelon's king was similarly deposed and replaced with one who would yield to Assyria. As for Ekron, likely nudged along by the urgings of Egypt, it had forcibly removed its king Padi and handed him over to Hezekiah for watchful care. However, the Egyptian support quickly failed and Ekron was quickly subdued. Those who lead the coup against Padi were gruesomely and publicly executed.

The final phase of Sennacherib's campaign focused upon Judah, and the results were devastating. According to Sennacherib's annals, 46 walled cities with their surrounding cities were overrun. In fact, such a claim comports well with the general archaeological data of the region.[14] In particular, Lachish, one of Judah's main administrative centers, took the brunt of the Assyrian efforts, which was vividly memorialized by Sennacherib's golden reliefs that eventually came to decorate his palace in Nineveh.[15]

9. Grayson and Novotny, *The Royal Inscriptions*, 169

10. Pallis, *The Antiquity of Iraq*, 70

11. Robb Andrew Young, *Hezekiah in History and Tradition* (VTSupp 155; Leiden: Brill, 2012), 77. Young gives this spectrum as a "generous estimate."

12. Young goes further when he suggests the timing represented an opportune moment as Sennacherib had recently lost key territories. Young, *Hezekiah in History*, 78.

13. Elayi, *Sennacherib*, 52–88.

14. Ephraim Stern, *Archaeology of the Land of the Bible: Volume II* (The Anchor Bible Reference Library; New York: Doubleday, 2001), 3–13, esp. 10; 130–215, esp. 130–31.

15. Lachish's destruction was studied most definitively by David Ussishkin in the

Yet when it came to Jerusalem, it did not fall. Sennacherib only claimed to have 1) locked Hezekiah up like a caged bird and 2) received tribute from Hezekiah after the fact.

How did the third campaign come to an end has been the subject of intense debate. Important to this discussion is reconstructing the events of the Battle at Eltekeh, the battle where the Egyptian Taharqa ostensibly faced off against Sennacherib. The critical question is simple. Did this encounter happen before or after the siege of Jerusalem? If it happened after the siege of Jerusalem, then this may explain why Sennacherib's account of his third military campaign ends rather abruptly. However, Robb Andrew Young has argued persuasively against seeing the Battle of Eltekeh as the reason for why the third military campaign ended the way that it did.[16] In particular, all the sources that speak of Sennacherib's third military campaign are unified in the notion that the campaign stopped due to something other than standard conventions of warfare.[17] According to Young, what ended the campaign was the stalwart defiance of a brilliant strategist, king Hezekiah of Judah. Sennacherib's third military campaign ended without the sacking of Jerusalem because the Assyrian king realized that the efforts and resources required to successfully overrun the city ran the risk of exposing his army to natural elements and/or losing the morale of his army.[18]

The Implications of the Taylor Prism

At the most basic level, the Taylor Prism adds another layer to the complexity of recounting the events of 701 BCE. For starters, 2 Kgs 18:17–20:19 is repeated in Is 36–39 and recast in 2 Chr 32, which poses questions of relationship and literary dependence within the Old Testament.[19] In addition, there

1970s. See David Ussishkin, *The Renewed Archaeological Excavations at Lachish (1973–1994), Volumes I–V* (Monographs of the Institute OF Archaeology 22; Tel Aviv: Tel Aviv University, 2004).

16. Young, *Hezekiah in History,* 81–84. Also, Elayi, *Sennacherib,* 67.

17. Young, *Hezekiah in History,* 83.

18. Young, *Hezekiah in History,* 83. Young points to several widely attested, non-combat reasons for a siege army to break off its target, including natural disasters, disease, lack of supplies, and low morale.

19. When it comes to the Chronicler's account, Hays admits a strong ideological impetus behind the recasting of the siege. However, the Chronicler's focus upon the Davidic dynasty in Jerusalem does not mean there is no historical value in the account. Hays, *Hidden Riches,* 227.

is essentially a positive and negative account within 2 Kgs 18-19. Second Kgs 18:13–16 *negatively* remembers Sennacherib's siege, as a time when Hezekiah capitulated to the Assyrian forces and stripped the temple treasuries in order to appease Assyrian demands. This is in stark contrast to 2 Kgs 18:17–19:37, so much so that some have sought to reconstruct multiple Assyrian campaigns to Judah.[20] Finally, many scholars believe that 2 Kgs 18:17–19:37 is the result of a literary process that conflated two, one independent traditions. According to such a scheme, one tradition focused on the Assyrian Rabshakeh and the other upon Hezekiah. Together, these once separate traditions preserve different vantage points of the same event.

Consequently, the Taylor Prism muddies the waters by not only adding a non-Israelite perspective, but also adding a perspective that appears to support the more negative account of 2 Kgs 18:13–16. Sennacherib boasts that he

> " . . . surrounded and conquered 46 of [Hezekiah's] fortified cities, fortresses, and smaller settlements and their environs, which were without number . . . . brought out of them 200,150 people, young and old, male and female, horses, mules, donkeys, camels and oxen, sheep and goats, which were without number, and I counted them as booty. As for him (Hezekiah), I confined him inside the city Jerusalem, his royal city, like a bird in a cage . . . As for him, Hezekiah, the fear of my lordly brilliance overwhelmed him and, after my (departure) he had the auxiliary forces and his elite troops whom he brought inside to strengthen the city Jerusalem, his royal city, and who had provided support, along with talents of gold, 800 talents of silver, choice antinomy, large blocks of ??, ivory beds, armchairs of ivory, elephant hides, elephant ivory, ebony, boxwood, every kind of valuable treasure, as well as his daughters, his palace women, male singers and female singers brought to Nineveh, my capital city, and he sent a mounted messenger of his to me to deliver this payment and to do obeisance."[21]

---

20. Most notably among biblical scholars, John Bright, *A History of Israel* (4th ed.; Louisville, KY: Westminster John Knox, 2000), 298–309. However, Young points to a number of issues against such a reconstruction: 1) the witness of the Assyrian sources; 2) the archaeological record; 3) the questionable nature of the fourteenth year synchronism; 4) the chronology of the Babylonian envoys; 5) the narratival implications for the transition between 2 Kgs 18:16 and 18:17. See Young, *Hezekiah in History*, 66–73, with bibliography for the debate on 66, n.10. Also, see Elayi, *Sennacherib*, 85–87.

21. Grayson and Novotny, *The Royal Inscriptions*, 176–77.

At this point, one is inclined to throw their hands up in frustration. How can one understand the relationship between all these vantage points? *Is* there a relationship? Can they be explained or synthesized? I believe they can be synthesized, but articulating a synthesis is not easy. It requires that one considers naturally occurring ambiguities in language.

In the previous chapter I suggested that understanding ancient history requires nuance. More specifically, in discussing the implications of the Tel Dan Stele I suggested that the conventions of ancient Near Eastern royal literature needed to be considered, especially when discussing the convergences of specific historical claims made by the Old Testament and extra-biblical voices. Understanding convergences requires the reader to be sensitive to the semantic demands and possibilities of the texts in question. But what does this commitment to the semantic demands look like? Perhaps a quick exercise will help clarify.)

Consider the statement, "Jerusalem was sacked in 586 BCE." On the surface, it may seem definitive and precise. However, *who* sacked Jerusalem? *Who* was the agent responsible? There is no explicit statement of agency. Of course, this can be clarified rather quickly by adding a phrase or clause that denotes agency. "Jerusalem was sacked in 586 BCE *by Nebuchadnezzar and the Neo-Babylonian Empire.*" But without explicit qualification different agencies may be imported onto any statement such as this.

Probing even deeper into the statement, "Jerusalem was sacked in 586 BCE," there is the question of *why* it was sacked. Again, one could tackle any semantic imprecision by merely adding phrases or clauses. Nevertheless, as the statement currently sits there could be a theological reason for the sacking of Jerusalem, say because of the systematic and continual rejection of the covenant. Yet there can also be political reasons, say because of Judah's incessant defiance of their suzerain Babylon. Both are legitimate answers to the question of *why* Jerusalem was sacked, and both are not necessarily mutually exclusive.

The point is this. Language can be elusive, and there will always be a certain level of ambiguity inherent to any statement. Furthermore, some types of statements will yield greater ambiguities than others. For example, poetic statements tend to be more semantically ambiguous than narrative statements. Therefore, to what extent linguistic ambiguity is curbed depends on several factors, including genre, qualification, authorial intentions, and others.

When it comes to ancient royal literature, it feeds off semantic ambiguity. This type of literature uses statements that appear clear, but without important qualifications they become contexts for half-truths. This suggests that the most fruitful syntheses will happen where the ambiguities inherent to language and literature are not immediately silenced. Rather, ambiguities are allowed to exist. If one is too quick to silence naturally occurring ambiguities, they run the risk of creating a false dichotomy that forces one to choose "one side or the other." As if to say, "Whose side are you on? Team Bible, or Team Archaeology?" Such an "either/or" scenario not only has significant apologetic implications but fails to properly consider the full dynamics of God's revelation.

Perhaps I can close with a few questions designed to get one thinking about the semantic demands and possibilities in the hope that a synthesis between the Old Testament and the Taylor Prism can be imagined. Is it possible that the miracle of 2 Kgs 18–19 exists in the fact that Jerusalem stood while everything around it was utterly decimated by the most effective and efficient war machine on the planet? Could it be that the quintessential proof of the Lord's favor for Judah and the Davidic dynasty was that Jerusalem, with its temple, was not burnt to an ash heap and that its dynastic family endured? What if the fact that Hezekiah eventually paid tribute to Assyria was a peripheral point acknowledged by the biblical historian on the way to making what was perceived to be a more important point? What if by including the short notification of Hezekiah's tribute at the onset of the account the historian was recognizing a fact of history while intentionally steering the narrative in another direction?

It seems that the biblical historian wanted to celebrate the cosmic king—Yahweh—in such a fashion that emphasized his cosmic protection of Jerusalem against the diabolical forces that sought to threaten his people. For Sennacherib, he too was confronted with the historical reality that Jerusalem remained standing. Consequently, his historians emphasized the destruction of Jerusalem's surroundings, which included Judah's second most important city, and the eventual tribute of Hezekiah. And because this climaxed the record of his third military campaign, Sennacherib's annals seek to deflect the most glaring criticism of his campaign—the king failed to sack the epicenter of the anti-Assyrian alliance in the southern Levant.

Consequently, in both the Hebrew and Assyrian accounts, the dynamics of ancient history writing are put on display—a concern for an accurate account of the past balanced with a specific point or message to be made for the sake of the audience. More importantly, both the Tel Dan Stele and the Taylor Prism force us to reckon with the Old Testament's veracity in unique ways. Yet make no mistake, any question about the Old Testament's veracity is intimately wedded to its literariness. In other words, any assessment of the Old Testament' veracity, and thus its authority, requires a literary awareness. The Old Testament is literature, it's *ancient* literature, and we can't ask it to bear a weight that it is not designed to bear. The difficulty is that such a pursuit often imparts a level of discomfort. "What do you mean that history writing is more than just the rote regurgitation of facts? What do you mean there is subjectivity, selectivity, artistry, and purpose inherent to history writing? And what do you mean that I need to consider all of them when trying to figure out the authoritative claims of Scripture?" The beauty of archaeology is that its finds often force us to engage these realities anew when we think we have it all figured out.

8

Kuntillet Ajrud

There are a number of things an archaeologist considers when he or she is trying to determine where to excavate. One consideration is travel routes. Find a travel route—better yet find the intersection of travel routes—and you will likely find a location that yields large amounts of material culture, which is the life blood of archaeological discourse.

Travel routes bisected Syria-Palestine. In fact, there is a wonderful resource written by David Dorsey called *The Roads and Highways of Ancient Israel*.[1] Dorsey offers details on a host of travel routes that cut across the landscape of Syria-Palestine. North, south, east, west through the most arid and inhospitable places. Yes, even the Sinai Peninsula. And in the northeast corner of that barren wilderness, at the crossroads of intersecting ancient travel routes and near a regional wadi, there is a spot that has proven to be one of the most formative sites for understanding popular conceptions of Yahweh during the period of the divided monarchy—Kuntillet Ajrud.

The Site

Kuntillet Ajrud sits approximately 50 kilometers south of Kadesh Barnea and about 15 kilometers west of Darb el-Gazza. Sitting along a significant travel route that took travelers from the Negev deep into Sinai and on toward Elat, Kuntillet Ajrud enjoys proximity to a regional wadi, Wadi Quraiya. Yet there is nothing overly imposing about Kuntillet Ajrud.

It was first explored by Sir Edward Palmer in the latter half of the nineteenth century. According to Zeʾev Meshel, who would formally excavate the site in the mid-1970s, Palmer found a small incised inscription that was

1. David A. Dorsey, *The Roads and Highways of Ancient Israel* (The ASOR Library of biblical and Near Eastern Archaeology; Baltimore: The Johns Hopkins University Press, 1991).

111

incidentally misinterpreted.[2] However, this find would prove to be prophetic, as Kuntillet Ajrud is famous for its inscriptions above all else. Subsequent exploration and excavation were sporadic. Musil visited the site in the early twentieth century, and Beno Rothenberg visited the site in the wake of the Six Day War. According to Meshel, Rothenberg was intrigued enough to identify the site as an Israelite site, but his interest soon waned.[3] It was not until the 1975–76 that Kuntillet Ajrud was excavated with any rigor and sustained enthusiasm. Meshel's excavations spanned three seasons.

Meshel identified two main structures along the top of the narrow, east-west oriented tel, and both structures exhibited the same general rectangular shape. However, the western most structure was more prominent in size and better preserved than the other. The larger structure was roughly 15 x 25 meters with 4 small rooms projecting out from each corner. Entry was obtained through a passage on the east side of the building, through a courtyard lined with benches. From the courtyard, visitors passed through a long, north-south oriented, narrow "bench room" on their way to the main courtyard, which contained several cooking facilities. There were other storage facilities off the main courtyard as well. Based on the flaking on the floor, many of the walls appeared to have been covered with white plaster, which was diversely decorated.

The smaller structure was poorly preserved. White plaster also seems to have covered its walls, but the general layout in comparison to the other building is impossible to determine.

The function of the buildings has attracted some debate. For example, the four, small, corner rooms projecting off the main edifice suggest to some that the site was a military outpost. However, Meshel argues that the site boasts no other architecture that is typical of fortification.[4] André Lemaire has suggested that the site was an administrative center that

2. Ze'ev Meshel, "Kuntillet Ajrud," *ABD*, 4:103

3. Meshel, "Kuntillet Ajrud," 4:103.

4. Meshel notes a lack of a casemate wall. Meshel, "Kuntillet Ajrud," 4:103. However, Dever mentions the presence of a casemate wall and describes the building as "a rather typical Iron Age Judean desert fort." William Dever, *Did God Have a Wife? Archaeology and Folk Religion in Ancient Israel* (Grand Rapids: William B. Eerdmans, 2005), 160; idem, *The Lives of Ordinary People in Ancient Israel: Where Archaeology and the Bible Intersect* (Grand Rapids: William B. Eerdmans, 2012), 263. The lack of consistency with other Judean fortresses is also noted by Meindert Dijkstra, "I have Blessed you by YHWH of Samaria and his Asherah: Texts with Religious Elements from the Soil Archive of Ancient Israel" in *Only One God? Monotheism in Ancient Israel and the Veneration of the Goddess Asherah* (eds. Bob Becking, *et. al.*; London: Sheffield Academic Press, 2001), 19.

trained a scribal class.[5] Still others suggest a cultic function based on the content of the inscriptions and the nature of the artwork.[6] While there are cultic implications associated with the artwork and epigraphy, a cultic function for the building is not the only explanation of the phenomena. In the end, it's best to leave the question open. However, there is a lot to be said for seeing this site as a caravansary, essentially an ancient truck stop, that served multiple functions.[7]

Whatever its function was, the site has proven to be epigraphically rich and generally fascinating. Several textile fragments of high-quality material were also found,[8] and pottery analysis of the site's assemblage has proven to be an important baseline for comparing and dating other pottery assemblages.[9] However, what carried the scholarly discussion were the inscriptions and artwork found there.

The Epigraphic and artistic finds at Kuntillet Ajrud

Meshel described several categories of inscriptions discovered at Kuntillet Ajrud.[10] First, there were incised inscriptions that were made both before and after firing. There were also ink inscriptions found on pottery and on the walls of the site's installations. In a related category, but one that Meshel separates, there was pictorial and decorative art found on the plaster covered walls, door jams and pottery, rendering images and motifs popular during the Iron Age. For example, there are representations of divine, human, and animal figures, performing a range of tasks. Some are playing

5. André Lemaire, *Les écoles et la formation de Bible dans l'ancien Israel* (OBO 39; Freibourg: Editions Universitaires; Göttingen: Vandenhoeck & Ruprecht, 1981), 30.

6. Dijkstra also acknowledges this connection. Meindert Dijkstra, "I have Blessed you," 22–23. For advocates of a religious center, the most notable is the excavator. Meshel, "Kuntillet Ajrud," 4:108–09.

7. See Dever, *The Lives of Ordinary People*, 263. Dever recognizes a militaristic and cultic function inherent to the site. "The site is thus a fort, but it also served quite sensibly as a sort of "inn"; and it had, as other sites did, and indisputable "gate shrine." Also, Dever, *Did God Have a Wife?*, 160. However, Hadley, for example, seems content with the idea of caravansary, generally defined. Judith M. Hadley, "Some Drawings and Inscriptions on Two Pithoi from Kuntillet Ajrud," *VT* 37.2 (1987): 207–208.

8. Meshel, "Kuntillet Ajrud," 4:106.

9. Dever describes this site as a "one-period site" with an assemblage firmly places in an Iron Age context. Dever, *Did God Have a Wife?*, 160; idem, *Lives of Ordinary People*, 263.

10. For a useful discussion, see Meshel, "Kuntillet Ajrud," 4:106–07.

musical instruments, and others are assuming what appears to be positions of worship. Many, if not all, appear to be cultic in nature. In fact, the relationship between the artwork and the inscriptions has been a point of significant discussion (see below).

Found were two large storage jars eventually labeled Pithos A and Pithos B. They have attracted a lion's share of the debate largely because of the inscriptions that were found on them. But they have also attracted debate because they exhibit writing *and* artwork. Naturally, the question arises how one is to understand a relationship between the two. Simply, are the writing and the artwork related? Many decline to see any meaningful relationship between the inscriptions and the artwork on Pithoi A and B, such as Judith Hadley, citing the overlap between the inscriptions and the artwork as well as the stylistic differences between individual strokes of the ink.[11] In one case, Dijkstra questions if the artwork and inscriptions were made on the pithoi before it was broken. Instead, in his mind, the inscriptions and artwork were "doodles" made by bored clerks who were working at the site.[12] All members of this camp essential agree, in the words of Hadley, that the pithoi are "the work of many different people."[13]

Brian Schimdt has bucked this trend, arguing in detail that the artwork and inscriptions are intimately connected.[14] He attempts to refute every argument against unity by appealing to artistic conventions, comparative examples, and spatial theory. He even thinks that both pithoi are meant to be understood in light of each other. In his mind, their "association of ideas," made possible by similar inscriptions, motifs, and images, suggests collaboration.[15] Pithos A and B represent a single composition with complimentary scenes.[16] More specifically, Pithos A emphasizes the imminence of the divine in an urban context and Pithos B the empty space aniconism in a rural worship context.

In the end, it's difficult to say with any certainty the relationship between the inscription and artwork on each pithoi, let along whether both

---

11. Hadley, "Some Drawings," 207.

12. Dijkstra, "I have Blessed you," 26.

13. Hadley, "Some Drawings," 207.

14. Brian B. Schmidt, "The Iron Age Pithoi Drawings from Horvat Teman or Kuntillet Ajrud: Some New Proposals," *JANER* 2 (2002): 91–125.

15. Schmidt, "The Iron Age Pithoi Drawings," 113–15.

16. Schmidt, "The Iron Age Pithoi Drawings," 115.

collaborate in such an intricate fashion, as Schmidt suggests. Nevertheless, Schmidt's proposal is very enticing.

When it comes to the inscriptions, P. Kyle McCarter's translation for the inscriptions of Pithos A and B is as good of a place to start as any. There is one inscription from Pithos A germane to the conversation, and two from Pithos B.

- Pithos A: Utterance of 'Ashyaw the king: "Say to Yehallel and to Yaw'asah and to [. . .]: 'I bless you by Yahweh of Samaria and his asherah!' "[17]

- Pithos B: Utterance of 'Amaryaw, "Say to my lord: 'Is it well with you? I bless you by Yahweh of Teman and his asherah. May he bless you and keep you, and may he be with my lord!' "[18]

- Pithos B: [. . .] to Yahweh of the Teman and his asherah. "And may he grant (?) everything that he asks from the compassionate god [. . .], and may he grant according to his needs all that he asks!"[19]

A few things immediately jump out from these translations. First is the fact that Yahweh is qualified by a geographic notation. There is "Yahweh of Samaria," the capital of Israel during the divided monarchy. There is also "Yahweh of Teman," which is town or region in Edomite territory just east of Kuntillet Ajrud.[20] However, it's not clear whether this implies any belief in the notion that Yahweh was known uniquely at each location, as if Yahweh of Samaria was different than Yahweh of Teman or Jerusalem or somewhere else. Second, the agent of blessing in each inscription is twofold, shown by McCarter's translation "Yahweh and his asherah." This phrase is the crux of the debate.

The phrase "and his asherah" stems from the consonants *waw-lamed-aleph-shin-resh-taw-hey*, and the first two consonants, *waw* and *lamed*, are a conjunction and preposition respectively. The term "asherah" is derived

---

17. "Kuntillet Ajrud: Inscribed Pithos A," translated by P. Kyle McCarter (*COS*, 2:171).

18. "Kuntillet Ajrud: Inscribed Pithos B," translated by P. Kyle McCarter (*COS*, 2:172).

19. "Kuntillet Ajrud: Inscribed Pithos B," 2:172.

20. Carl G. Rasmussen, *Zondervan Atlas of the Bible* (rev. ed.; Grand Rapids: Zondervan, 2010), 62. McCarter concurs, providing an alternate rendering as "Yahweh of the Southland." He even suggests that possibility that Yahweh of Teman was the "local form worshiped in the vicinity of Kuntillet Ajrud." *COS*, 2:172, n. 1.

from the consonants *aleph-shin-resh-taw*, which leaves the final consonant to be explained. To many, the final *hey* is interpreted as a possessive suffix. However, this conclusion is by no means universal, as we shall see momentarily. In the end, any conclusion hinges on a few considerations.

First, one must determine whether *aleph-shin-resh-taw* refers to a proper name or a more generic noun. If it's a proper name, referring to a well-known goddess in the Canaanite pantheon, then the reading of "Asherah" is preferred.[21] However, there is also the possibility that *aleph-shin-resh-taw* refers to a symbol representative of the goddess, probably a wood pole of some sort. This possibility has support in the biblical and iconographic traditions, and in such case, "asherah" is the preferred translation.[22] Yet it is also possible, although very difficult, that "asherah" refers to a symbolic representation of Yahweh, which would also suggest reading a generic noun.[23] If one is inclined to understand *aleph-shin-resh-taw* as a symbolic representation of either Yahweh or Asherah, then the final *hey* is most likely a possessive suffix.

The problem with understanding *aleph-shin-resh-taw* as a proper name, as "Asherah," is that it's grammatically difficult. As noted by so many, a possessive suffix fixed to a proper name is unprecedented within Biblical Hebrew. However, this has not detracted some commentators from seeing the final *hey* as a possessive suffix fixed onto a proper name. Gogel suggests that the inscriptions of Kuntillet Ajrud, and those of Khirbet el-Qom for that matter, preserve the earliest examples of such a phenomenon.[24] Yet the final *hey* may not refer to a possessive suffix at all,

21. The main source of information on the goddess Asherah comes from the Ugaritic texts (see chapter above). There, she is presented in a diverse manner, but there is a prevailing notion that she was a mother goddess and likely a consort of El, who was the chief god of the Canaanite pantheon. She is also an active character in the affairs of the pantheon. For example, she intercedes on behalf of Baal and seduces other gods. Asherah also appears to have regional representations, ranging from Egypt, through Syria-Palestine, and in Mesopotamia. See John Day, "Asherah (Deity)," *ABD*, 1:483–87; Nicolas Wyatt, "Asherah," *DDD*, 99–105.

22. Wyatt suggests that a cultic object is the most popular referent within the biblical tradition. Wyatt, "Asherah," 101.

23. Hess notes the difficult of such view, which hinges upon the notion that feminine qualities of the goddess were absorbed by Yahweh. See Hess's critique in Richard Hess, *Israelite Religions: An Archaeological and Biblical Survey* (Grand Rapids: Baker Academic, 2007), 287–88. For the idea explained, see Patrick D. Miller, *The Religion of Ancient Israel* (Library of Ancient Israel; Louisville: Westminster John Knox, 2000), 229–40.

24. Gogel, *Epigraphic Hebrew*, 156; 414–15. Schmidt is receptive to this, even citing evidence from related languages that show possessive suffixes fixed to proper nouns.

but rather a historical spelling attested outside of Israel but not used by Israelite writers. According to Richard Hess, "It is possible to render the goddess's name "Asheratah," in accordance with the spelling and reading of her name everywhere outside of the Bible for more than a thousand years."[25] More specifically, the final *hey* may be a "second feminine ending or a vowel letter reflecting a final *a* vowel."[26]

The Implications of the Inscriptions

Schmidt is correct to allude to the differences between Epigraphic Hebrew and Biblical Hebrew when trying to understand the inscriptions of Kuntillet Ajrud. Quite simply, the rules of Biblical Hebrew should not be automatically assumed upon an inscription that exhibits Epigraphic Hebrew.[27] Thus, reading a possessive suffix on a proper noun, "his Asherah," is not beyond the realm of possibility, particularly in light of the comparative evidence that may be marshalled. However, in my opinion, reading all the consonants *aleph-shin-resh-taw-hey* as a proper name is preferable. Like Hess, "Yahweh and Asherah" is arguably the best reading of the pithoi inscriptions.

Yet whether one reads "Asherah," "his Asherah," or "his asherah," the effect is essentially the same. These inscriptions are effectively invoking a blessing from two deities.[28] What's more, Yahweh is pitted alongside one

---

Schmidt, "The Iron Age Pithoi Drawings," 105.

25. Hess, *Israelite Religions*, 284. Also see Richard Hess, "Asherah or Asheratah?" *Orientalia* 65 (1996): 209–19.

26. Hess, *Israelite Religions*, 288. Hess invokes A. Angerstorfer, "Ašerah als 'consort of Jahwe' oder Aširtah? *BN* 17 (1982): 7–16 and Ziony Zevit, *The Religions of Ancient Israel: A Parallactic Approach* (New York: Continuum, 2001).

27. According to Soulen and Soulen, epigraphy is the "field of study concerned with the classification of and interpretation of inscriptions." Richard N. Soulen and R. Kendall Soulen, "Epigraphy" in *Handbook of Biblical Criticism* (3d. ed.; Louisville: Westminster John Knox, 2001), 53. Thus, Epigraphic Hebrew refers to the language of Hebrew inscriptions, which Gogel further defines by those that appeared between the 10th and 6th centuries BCE. Gogel, *Grammar of Epigraphic Hebrew*, 5. However, while Gogel and others, such as Angel Sáenz-Badillos, clearly acknowledge the relationship between Epigraphic and Biblical Hebrew, they are also aware of the differences. For a good historical description of the Hebrew Language, including Biblical Hebrew, Epigraphic Hebrew, and its neighbors, see Angel Sáenz-Badillos, *A History of the Hebrew Language* (trans. John Elwolde; Cambridge: Cambridge University Press, 1993).

28. If one interprets the consonants as a symbolic representation of the goddess and not the goddess herself, it still implies acknowledgement or and reliance upon the capabilities of the goddess.

of the chief goddesses of the Canaanite pantheon, a goddess whom the Old Testament targets on multiple occasions. But do these inscriptions mean that there was a prevailing belief that Yahweh had a consort, as many scholars have suggested? If one understands the final *hey* to be a possessive suffix on "Asherah," then the likelihood that this inscription reflects a belief that Asherah was Yahweh's wife increases significantly. Yet if the possessive suffix is read fixed on a generic noun, "his asherah," then likelihood of a consort is reduced. In this case, it's more likely that "his asherah" refers to a symbolic representation of Asherah closely linked to the worship of Yahweh. If the final *hey* is understood to be an archaic spelling of Asherah, "Asheratah," then there is still a possibility that a consort is in view, but it's neither necessary nor explicit. Such a conclusion must be inferred by means other than the grammar of the inscription.

For those who are familiar with the governing theology of the Old Testament, this body of evidence, and the entire discussion really, may be unsettling. Overall, the Canonical statement of the Old Testament advocates strict separation between Yahweh and the deities of Israel's cultural environment. Moreover, when it comes to the deities of the Canaanites, there is particular disdain (e.g. Deut 7:5–6; 12:2–4; 1 Kgs 14:22–24; 17:16). In fact, the separation is so dramatic that at certain points the Old Testament overtly questions the existence of other deities (e.g. Deut 4:35; Is 46:1–13). Consequently, the idea that Israelites may have put Yahweh alongside pagan deities, or even believed that Yahweh was so closely associated with them that marriage was the most effective metaphor, seems to fly in the face of the Old Testament. However, instead of seeing the inscriptions of Kuntillet Ajrud as something hostile to the message of the Old Testament, it's more appropriate to understand the data as a reinforcement of its message.

Religious syncretism is arguably the biggest concern voiced by the Old Testament. For example, Deut 7:1–6 informs the reader that even the threat of syncretism was serious, and so serious that it had to be met with drastic measures. Because the religious tendencies of the indigenous Canaanites threatened to incur the wrath of the Lord and threaten the holiness of the people, the sheer presence of the people groups along with their religious instruments were to be eradicated. Unfortunately, the biblical legislation failed to deter, for the prophets continuously railed against the syncretistic practices of the people. For example, the oracles of Jeremiah (19:3–13) and Ezekiel (8:9–18) call out specific practices occurring at all levels of society. Then there is the classic account of Elijah taking on the prophets of Baal, urging the populace to pick a side in the process (1 Kgs 18). Kuntillet Ajrud, therefore, is extra-biblical evidence that reinforces the validity of the prophetic critique and the general concern of the Old Testament.

I close with a quote from Hess on the significance of the Kuntillet Ajrud inscriptions.

> "[T]he texts have provided what is arguably the major catalyst for a revolution in our understanding of the beliefs of the Israelites during the monarchy . . . It is, in fact, no longer possible to accept a simple division between those who worshipped Yahweh as a single and unique deity, on the one hand, and those who served Baal and a pantheon of deities, on the other."[29]

Among the general populace it's difficult to perceive a sharp dichotomy between those who worshiped Yahweh exclusively and/or properly with those who worshipped him alongside other pagan gods and goddesses. Whether from the evidence of Kuntillet Ajrud, other sites such as Khirbet el-Qom, or from the overall cultural footprint of Israel and Judah that exhibits a diverse repertoire of forms and symbols, the lines were blurred. Diversity was the theological milieu of the prophets.

29. Hess, *Israelite Religions*, 283.

9

The Ketef Hinnom Amulets

In the summer of 2016, the excavators of Ashkelon announced the discovery a Philistine cemetery.[1] The importance of this find can be articulated in a variety of ways, but for the purposes of this chapter, let's begin with the reality that people in antiquity were often buried with a wide variety of "stuff." Yet before we wrinkle our noses at the thought of being interned with jewelry, clothes, weapons, even other people, we should recognize that the differences between ancient and modern people might not be as wide as we first think. Whether a favorite hat that supports a favorite team, a valued possession, or something else, people today are still buried with "stuff." Moreover, those things reveal something about that person and what he or she valued. Thus, the burial practices of humanity display certain points of commonality across cultures and centuries and function as an important area of study.

The ancient Israelites were also buried with "stuff." Naturally then, excavations of Israelite burial sites are potentially fruitful. In fact, in the late 1970s, the burial site of Ketef Hinnom lived up to this potentiality. There, archaeologists found a burial complex filled with copious small finds that dated to the late seventh and early sixth centuries BCE. These would have been significant by themselves, as anything that illuminates Judean culture immediately before the Babylonian invasions is noteworthy, but two tiny silver scrolls were excavated, which launched the importance of the site to an entirely different level.

---

1. This was reported on numerous outlets. For example, Kristin Romey, "Discovery of Philistine Cemetery may Solve Biblical Mystery, *National Geographic*, July 10, 2016, https://news.nationalgeographic.com/2016/07/bible-philistine-israelite-israel-ashkelon-discovery-burial-archaeology-sea-peoples/ (accessed January 25, 2019).

The Site and the Finds

Ketef Hinnom, "shoulder of Hinnom," refers to a rocky hill that sits about 80 meters above the Hinnom valley that runs across the western side of ancient Jerusalem. Ketef Hinnom exhibits at least 7 burial caves and is known to have been a part of a larger burial complex that spanned the larger ridgeline that overlooks the Hinnom Valley. Of those burial caves on Ketef Hinnom, a couple are quite complex. Gabriel Barkay notes that two burial caves were "multi-chambered," with a total of fifteen burial chambers having been identified between the two.[2]

One of those burial chambers, named Chamber 25, measured approximately 3.3 x 2.9 meters and exhibited 3 benches fixed to the cave walls. These benches were likely used for the initial internment, or burial, of a corpse. One of those benches was observed to be "unusually broad" with cutouts most likely for the placement of the heads of the deceased.[3] Beneath the unusually wide bench was an undisturbed repository. It measured at its maximum width approximately 3.7 x 2 meters and, when excavated, it contained the remains of approximately 100 people and over 1000 items.[4] From pottery, to coins, to the two silver scrolls, the content of this repository signaled not only a lengthy period of usage but also the significant wealth for those buried there.

The silver scrolls were discovered inside the repository. Scroll 1 was found in the debris approximately 7 centimeters above the repository's floor. Scroll 2 was found while sifting the repository's debris. In the case of the former, its relative closeness to the floor suggested to Barkay its relative antiquity, which was later confirmed by the paleographic analysis of the scroll.[5]

Rolled, each of the scrolls essentially looked like a burnt cigarette butt. Scroll 1 measured approximately 27 millimeters in length and 11 millimeters in diameter with scroll 2 measuring approximately 11.5 mm x 5.5 mm.[6] Unrolled, scroll 1 reached approximately 97 millimeters in length, but

---

2. Gabriel Barkay, "The Priestly Benediction on Silver Plaques from Ketef Hinnom in Jerusalem," *TA* 19.2 (1992): 141. I rely upon the *editio princeps* for many details in this description.

3. Barkay, "The Priestly Benediction," 143.

4. Barkay, "The Priestly Benediction," 145.

5. Barkay, "The Priestly Benediction," 148.

6. Barkay, "The Priestly Benediction," 148.

scroll 2 only about 39 millimeters.[7] Consequently, to say that these scrolls were small would be something of an understatement. Making things more difficult, the scrolls cracked and broke while being unrolled, rendering the poorly preserved letters virtually impossible to read. Nevertheless, with enough patience, microscope power, and the best photography available to date, scholars were able to discern enough to suggest a coherent message based on the so-called Priestly Blessing found in Numb 6:24–26.

In his *editio princeps*, Barkay offered the following readings.

- Scroll 1: "Bless you Yahweh [and k]eep you may Yahweh shine [his f]ac[e upon you and be gracious to you]."[8]

- Scroll 2: "Bless you Yahweh and keep you may shine Yahweh his face upon you and give you peace."[9]

Metallurgical analysis determined that the scrolls were composed of 99% silver and 1% copper, which Barkay described as "undoubtedly deliberate."[10] But perhaps more fascinating is the conclusion by Barkay that the scrolls were written by two different hands, in what was called a "vulgar script," dated to the second half of the seventh century BCE.[11] This implies that literacy and scribal abilities were enjoyed by privileged parts of the Judean populace shortly before the Babylonian Exile.

The method by which the scrolls were unrolled was very complex. When researchers realized that unrolling the scrolls by hand would ensure their destruction, they first tried applying a saline solution mixed with 30% formic acid over a period of several months.[12] Some headway was made, but researchers soon abandoned this effort due to significant cracking and breaking. Success was ultimately achieved when the researchers applied an acrylic glue, Plextol B500, a popular compound used for the conservation of fragile materials.[13] With the aid of a sharp stylist, the scrolls were delicately unrolled and presented for analysis.

---

7. Barkay, "The Priestly Benediction," 149–50.

8. Barkay, "The Priestly Benediction," 160.

9. Barkay, "The Priestly Benediction," 167.

10. Barkay, "The Priestly Benediction," 174.

11. Barkay, "The Priestly Benediction," 169; 174.

12. Marina Rasovsky, David Bigelajzen, and Dodo Shenhav, "Cleaning and Unrolling the Silver Plaques," *TA* 19.2 (1992): 192–94.

13. Rasovsky, Bigelajzen, and Shenhav, "Cleaning and Unrolling," 193.

When Barkay first published the content of the scrolls in 1992, he was hard pressed to find any coherence in the opening lines of the scrolls. He tentatively identified the consonants *yodh-hey-waw* and considered them to be a theophoric element in someone's name.[14] Yet outside of this, Barkay could only offer a string of consonants and speculate on the sense of the text. However, beginning in line 14 he was able to read a version of the so-called priestly blessing from Numbers 6. For scroll 2, the situation was similar—a sequence of lines appeared to quote the priestly benediction of Numbers 6, but beyond these lines the consonants made little sense.

One year prior, Ada Yardeni spoke to these difficulties. She discussed how she was asked to examine and draw the text. In the process of her discussion, she emphasized the need for a microscope and other magnifying tools.[15] Nevertheless, despite the difficulties of the texts, Yardeni remained certain enough to declare the "crystallization" of the priestly blessing during the latter part of the seventh century BCE.[16] Consequently, these laments, as well as the reality that scrolls went undeciphered for over a decade after their initial discovery, gave credence to the need to find and develop new technologies, or at least apply old technologies in new way, so that the content of the scrolls could be read more confidently. That moment came early in the 2000s.

Barkay teamed up with the West Semitic Research Project (abbr. WSRP) at the University of Southern California to apply different photographic technologies to the surface of the scrolls in the hope that the content could be deciphered more effectively. Lighting was the most critical factor.

14. Barkay, "The Priestly Benediction," 154.

15. Ada Yardeni, "Remarks on the Priestly Blessing on Two Amulets from Jerusalem," *VT* 41.2 (1991): 176.

16. Yardeni, "Remarks on the Priestly Blessing," 181.

So, armed with new developments in fiber optics, the team employed an age-old method of "light painting," only with a twist.[17] Other important considerations were those of verification, the cracks in the scrolls, and the reconstruction of faint or partially formed letters. Template letters were used to verify and reconstruct suspect letters, and "patching" was employed to extend strokes across gaps created by the breaks in the scrolls. Also, high resolution scans of the copious pictures taken were read through very advanced digital platforms to verify reconstructed readings. Yet without a doubt, it was the graphic software and innovative applications that allowed the team to decipher the texts with more confidence. And in the end, many of Barkay's initial theories were supported, including the function of the scrolls as amulets and a seventh century dating.

Nevertheless, Barkay and company did experience some pushback. For example, Johannes Renz argued against a seventh century date for the composition of the scrolls.[18] Renz argued that the archaeological context of the finds and the script suggested a Hellenistic period for the scrolls, not an Iron II context. In particular, Renz noted several linguistic features as evidence for dating the composition of the scrolls later. Those features include the forms of certain letters, the presence of internal consonantal vowels, the construction of the third person masculine singular pronominal suffix on certain nominal forms, and the pronominal suffix form on a *beth* preposition. However, Barkay and company answered each one of these points systematically in 2004.[19] First, they took serious issue with Renz's understanding of the stratigraphy.[20] Indeed, there was material in the repository that dated to the Hellenistic period; it was a grave complex used during that period. But the Hellenistic material was significantly removed from the layering in which the scrolls were found. Next, Barkay and company questioned how much stock one should put in Renz's linguistic and orthographic arguments. The new photographs published in 2003 in *Near Eastern Archaeology* cast serious doubt on Renz's conclusions regarding the

17. For the sophisticate details, Gabriel Barkay, *et. al.*, "The Challenges of Ketef Hinnom: Using Advanced Technologies to Reclaim the Earliest Biblical Texts and their Context," *NEA* 66.4 (2003): 164–66.

18. Johannes Renz, *Handbuch der althebräschen Epigraphik* (3 vols; Darmstadt: Wissenschaftliche Buchgesellschaft, 1995), 1:447–56.

19. Gabriel Barkay, *et. al.*, "The Amulets from Ketef Hinnom: A New Edition and Evaluation," *BASOR* 334 (2004): 41–71.

20. Barkay, *et. al.*, "The Amulets from Ketef Hinnom," 43.

form of certain letters.[21] Second, the script should be characterized as a vulgar script and shows signs on inconsistency. And if a script is inconsistent with its features, then how much stock can one put into it as absolute support for a Hellenistic date?

In the end, Barkay and company were more convinced than ever that Barkay's initial ideas were largely correct. Accepting this, the Ketef Hinnom scrolls constitute the earliest known citations of the Old Testament literary tradition. In what follows are the readings offered by Barkay and company at the end of the 2004 article.

- Scroll 1: " . . . YHW . . . the grea[t . . . who keeps] the covenant and [G]raciousness toward those who love [him] and those who keep [his commandments . . .]. The Eternal (?) . . . [the] blessing more than any [sna]re and more than Evil. For redemption is in him. For Yahweh is our restorer [and] rock. May Yahweh bles[s] you and [may he] keep you. [May] Yahweh make [his face] shine . . . "[22]

- Scroll 2: "[For PN, the son/daughter of PN]. May h[e]/sh[e] be blessed by Yahweh, the warrior [or, helper] and the rebuke of [E]vil: May Yahweh bless you, keep you. May Yahweh make his face shine upon you and grant you p[ea]ce."[23]

If this is correct, does it follow that the scrolls exist as evidence for dating elements of the biblical text? It's with this question that the implications of the Ketef Hinnom scrolls come into view.

The Implications of the Ketef Hinnom Amulets

In 2002, Erik Waaler discussed the implications for dating the priestly traditions in light of the Ketef Hinnom scrolls.[24] Ever since Julius Wellhausen's classic articulation of the sources behind the Pentateuch, the tendency has been to date the composition of the priestly traditions to the era after the exile. Indeed, there have been detractors to Wellhausen's ideas, but they have always been in the minority. According to Waaler, however, these

21. Barkay, *et. al.*, "The Amulets from Ketef Hinnom," 50.

22. Barkay, *et. al.*, "The Amulets from Ketef Hinnom," 61.

23. Barkay, *et. al.*, "The Amulets from Ketef Hinnom," 68.

24. Erik Waaler, "A Revised Date for Pentateuchal Texts?: Evidence from Ketef Hinnom," *TyndBul* 53.1 (2002): 29–54.

scrolls constitute empirical evidence that cuts across traditional scholarly assumptions and forces a fundamental reconsideration.

First and foremost, according to Waaler, the linguistic similarities between the scrolls and Numb 6:24–26 are so profound that they point to the existence of a valued and standardized tradition informing both Numbers and the scrolls.[25] Waaler does not believe such similarities would be possible otherwise. More precisely, Waaler points to the identical presence of the internal vowels between the biblical and non-biblical texts as evidence for a "common archetype."[26] Second, scroll 2 shortens the priestly blessing and alludes to Deut 7:9 as well.[27] Consequently, Waaler ponders another "common archetype." In other words, Waaler believes that the scrolls are pulling from source texts that would also eventually produce the books of Numbers and Deuteronomy. As to the nature of the source text, Waaler speculates that it was likely longer, more complex, and cultic in nature, which stands in contrast to the scrolls as amulets.[28]

Perhaps the boldest element of his thesis is how Waaler reconstructs a history of development for the archetypes. Because the scrolls are dated by their writing style to the seventh century BCE, Waaler argues that it's necessary to proceed further back for a context of composition as the source texts needed an appropriate time to develop as a written tradition and gain the necessary credibility to be used as an amulet. Ultimately, Waaler is content with seeing a context of composition for the common archetypes dated to Josiah or Manasseh's day.[29]

Waaler seems convinced that there scrolls constitute hard evidence that the priestly traditions and the Deuteronomic traditions were being composed in large order during the seventh century BCE or before. But do they? I think that Waaler is on the right track to consider the implications of the Ketef Hinnom scrolls, but in my opinion, I think things need to be framed more precisely. These scrolls *by themselves* do not constitute direct evidence for any large-scale composition of the biblical material. The only thing that these scrolls directly evince is that people were invoking and inscribing small, mnemonic portions of the priestly traditions—not direct evidence for any large-scale composition.

25. Waaler, "A Revised Date," 44.
26. Waaler, "A Revised Date," 47–48.
27. Waaler, "A Revised Date," 49–51.
28. Waaler, "A Revised Date," 51–53.
29. Waaler, "A Revised Date," 53–54.

At this point, it's important to make a distinction between the Old Testament texts and the traditions, written and oral, that would come to inform and make up the Old Testament. The reality is that the Old Testament became a corpus through a lengthy process of textualization,[30] and many of the accounts that would become the Old Testament were preserved orally and only later through a lengthy and complicated written process. Even in the cases when the material behind the Old Testament bypassed any oral stage of existence and was written down immediately, there was still a process of preservation and development before it came to the form seen in the Old Testament. Thus, any discussion about the compositional history of the Old Testament must be nuanced enough to accommodate a host of social, historical, and cultural variables.

So, if we look at these scrolls in the context of these other variables, such as the development of Judean culture in Iron II, they bear testimony to a broader cultural context that was conducive to the large-scale composition of the biblical traditions, which included the priestly traditions. In other words, the Ketef Hinnom scrolls by themselves only offer partial evidence for the large-scale composition of the Old Testament. Taken in a larger context, their significance is more robust.

It is critical that we appreciate finds like these for what they offer. When we engage is sensationalized banter, we are often humbled, perhaps even humiliated. In the case of Ketef Hinnom, we see some of the earliest quotations of the Old Testament traditions as well as one of the earliest invocations of Yahweh. When it comes to the priestly traditions, it shows that they were established enough to be used by the populace. As for what this all means for Wellhausen's ideas, it means that the Ketef Hinnom scrolls contribute to the onslaught against the Documentary Hypothesis, *classically defined*, making it largely untenable. Moreover, the scrolls militate against any insistence that the priestly traditions are post-exilic compositions with post-exilic sources.[31]

---

30. Schniedewind has shown what the contours of such a process may have looked like. William Schniedewind, *How the Bible Became a Book, passim.* While the details can be debated, the general contours of development are beyond question.

31. In addition, it's also worth noting the sophisticated rituals found the Ugaritic and Emar tablets. This body of data testifies that some Israelite rituals have comparative precedence in the Bronze Ages cultures, thereby further supporting the possibility that the priestly traditions are rooted it the earliest stages of Israel's existence. See Hess, *Israelite Religions*, 95–122, with particular emphasis upon Emar, 112–23.

So, we can thank archaeology, which includes the finds at Ketef Hinnom, for the onslaught against any dogmatic stance that the priestly traditions are post-exilic. But going beyond the implications of when the biblical traditions may have been composed, the Ketef Hinnom scrolls also appear to shed some light on how the biblical traditions were used by the populace—as magical amulets used to ward off harmful spirits.

In 2012, Jeremy Smoak argued that the scrolls, particularly scroll 1, shed light on how incantations functioned apotropaically, as talismans to magically ward off evil.[32] Taking a lead from Barkay and company's 2004 article, Smoak emphasized that the scrolls likely had a magical function. In particular, Smoak argued that the structure and content of the scroll demonstrated affinities with other apotropaic amulets and inscriptions found across the ancient Near East. Moreover, Smoak connected specific verbs in the priestly blessing, such as to "guard" and to "bless," to other magical incantations found in the context surrounding Israel.[33] Thus, the content of the scroll suggests that "the deity will protect the wearer because he has been loyal to the commandments and because the deity's words are more powerful that Evil . . . [and the wearer] can expect to be protected because his amulet has been inscribed with an efficacious blessing associated with the temple."[34]

Smoak went on to structurally compare what he calls the petitionary psalms with the scroll. These psalms solicit the Lord's protection against adversaries often characterized as evil, wicked, or something similar. Ultimately, Smoak observes important parallels. "The fact that these prayers could be used to address such diverse ills parallels the nature of the incantation texts in the ancient Near East."[35] More specifically, Smoak highlights that the sentiment of affirmation often exhibited in these psalms is also paralleled in the Ketef Hinnom scroll by its succinct statements about the Lord and the introduction of the statements via the particle kî, כִּ.[36] Yet most importantly, Smoak argues that the close structural connections between the

32. Jeremy D. Smoak, "May Yhwh Bless You and Keep You from Evil: The Rhetorical Argument of Ketef Hinnom Amulet I and the Form of the Prayers for Deliverance in the Psalms," *JANER* 12 (2012): 202–36.

33. Smoak, "May Yhwh Bless You," 216.

34. Smoak, "May Yhwh Bless You," 219.

35. Smoak, "May Yhwh Bless You," 220.

36. Smoak, "May Yhwh Bless You," 224. Nevertheless, Smoak does not suggest that the forms and structures of incantation texts were overly rigid. Rather, the evidence suggests a certain amount of fluidity (p. 227).

scroll, certain psalms, and other incantation texts of the ancient Near East suggest an ideological closeness between liturgical texts and magical texts. Smoak believes there to be a functional and anthropological relationship, and both the psalms and incantations accomplished these goals in similar ways—ritual speech and ritual action.

Smoak's work rightly emphasizes the ideological connections between certain psalms, incantations, and magic. The affinities of content, structure, and syntax are hard to ignore, even though some of the examples offered by Smoak may not be precise. Yet the proposal is enough to raise certain questions about perceptions that informed the thought-world of ancient Israel, perceptions that undoubtedly influenced the writers of the biblical traditions. But to be clear, the specifics of that relationship are uncertain. For instance, do the connection between Ketef Hinnom, magic, and the psalms suggest some sort of historical relationship? Thus, Smoak is correct that more research is needed. Regardless, the Ketef Hinnom scrolls demonstrate how the general populace was using elements of the biblical traditions in the seventh century BCE. And in some cases, we see that the populace used elements of the biblical tradition in ways that were eventually frowned upon (cf. Deut 18:10–11; Is 3:18).[37]

37. However, Smoak questions the details of such opposition. Smoak, "May Yhwh Bless You," 228, n. 59.

10

Mt. Ebal

Archaeological research in Syria-Palestine has traditionally privileged the tel. Tels are mounds of dirt that enclose series of ancient settlements where phases of occupation pile upon previous phases of occupation. The result is something of a layered cake where the history of occupation and culture are detailed in the layers of dirt observable as one excavates the mound. And with so much history and occupation in one relatively contained location, it's no wonder why tels have been privileged.

However, the problem with such a preference is that a large portion of the population in ancient Israel, particularly within the boundaries of ancient Israel, lived outside major urban centers. So, while tels may offer the most amount of data in the smallest area, the countryside offers a valuable dynamic to constructing an exhaustive picture of ancient Israelite culture, history, and settlement. Such was the logic behind the great Manasseh survey that took place in the 1970s. A team of archaeologists that included Adam Zertal sought to survey about 1000 square miles by foot. Indeed, more than a modest task! Yet it was a critical task as such a survey would expose the Central Highlands, the region in which the earliest evidence for Israel has been found, to a much needed robust and systematic investigation.

In 1980, Zertal and his crew made their way up Mt. Ebal to el-Burnat, "the hat," a location that sits about 500 feet below Ebal's summit (about 3000 feet above sea level). Here Zertal observed a large stone structure, which was in turn excavated between 1982–89. What was discovered has proven to be one of the most polarizing finds in the history of archaeological research in Israel.

The Site and the Finds[1]

The site of Mt. Ebal shows a short period of occupation. The excavators observed only two strata of occupation, and the span of occupation reaches from approximately the middle of the thirteenth century to the end of the twelfth.[2] The earliest phase of occupation, Stratum II, was very modest, often described as a small village. Stratum I manifested a significant development of Stratum II and has been divided into two distinct sub-phases: IA and IB.[3]

Initially, two areas of excavation were opened.[4] Area A focused on the center of the site and its stone installation. Area B focused upon an observable rock line northwest of Area A. In Stratum II of Area B, Zertal and company found a building that was interpreted to be a 4-room pillared house built upon bedrock, apparently used by the individual or family that serviced the site. Inside, excavators unearthed a silo with a diverse pottery assemblage.[5]

The finds of Area A were significantly more complex. In Stratum II, a circular stone installation built upon bedrock was excavated. Dubbed Installation 94, this stone structure was about 6.5 feet in diameter and filled with about 4 inches of ash and a variety of animal bones.[6] Most interestingly, it sat directly below the center of the large stone installation of Stratum I. In the immediate vicinity, a pit, named Pit 250, was found to contain a substantial and diverse collection of tools and other implements, including pottery and chalices.[7] All things considered, Zertal and company suggested that Stratum II constituted a modest cultic site.[8]

---

1. We are indebted to Ralph Hawkins for his important monograph that synthesizes the myriad of publications regarding this site. Ralph K. Hawkins, *The Iron Age I Structure on Mt. Ebal: Excavation and Interpretation* (Winona Lake, IN: Eisenbrauns, 2012).

2. Hawkins says approximately 1140 BCE for the end of the site. Ralph Hawkins, *Joshua* (ECC; Bellingham, WA: Lexham Press, forthcoming).

3. Adam Zertal, "Ebal, Mount (Place)," *ABD* 2:255.

4. Area C would later be opened to investigate the site's northern most enclosure. Zertal, "Ebal, Mount (Place)," 2:255. Also Hawkins, *The Iron Age I Structure*, 49–53.

5. Hawkins, *The Iron Age I Structure*, 88–9; 38.

6. Hawkins, *The Iron Age I Structure*, 33

7. Hawkins, *The Iron Age I Structure*, 34

8. Adam Zertal, "An Early Iron Age Cultic Site on Mount Ebal: Excavation Seasons 1982–87," *TA* 13–14 (1986–87): 151.

Stratum I of Area A reveals the site's massive upgrade and development. Installation 94 was covered with a large, square stone structure, whose four corners touched the four points on a compass and whose dimension was approximately 29 x 23 feet.[9] Yet observable within the large stone structure was a dividing wall and a significant amount of fill comprised of layers of rŏck, dirt, ash, faunal remains, and pottery. In fact, this fill has proven to be a critical element in the discussions that seek to identify the function of the Mt. Ebal site (see below).

The excavators also observed a large ledge around the large stone installation as well as an ascending row of stones that was interpreted as a ramp up to the top of the main structure. Two courtyards flanked the ramp, and within them were several small stone installations filled with ash, pottery, faunal remains, and other discarded material. Proceeding further out from the large stone installation, a wall of approximately 3 feet in height and just over 800 feet long enclosed the area. And the apparent domicile of Stratum II Area B was paved over with smaller stones to create a courtyard and entry point for the main complex.

The top most layer of the site was interpreted as an intentional and systematic covering of the site. For advocates of the notion that Mt. Ebal was a large cult site, this layer of stone is interpreted as a phase of decommissioning for the site, which does have support from the larger cultural milieu.[10] For those who reject the notion that Mt. Ebal was a large Iron I cult site, these large stones are often interpreted as some type of natural field accumulation.

Other important finds at Ebal included a rich pottery assemblage that displays many affinities with typical "Israelite" forms, dating the early stages of Iron I.[11] But among this assemblage, there was a tellingly small number, but not absence, of known cooking vessels, which is odd for a site that has been interpreted as a village or some other type of domestic site. In addition, there were no sickle blades, a popular field working tool during the Iron Ages, and many flint knives and other small finds made from precious metals.[12] But without a doubt, the faunal remains are the most intriguing,

9. Hawkins notes precise dimensions: 28.7ft. x 30ft. x 23 ft. Hawkins, *The Iron Age I Structure*, 39.

10. Hawkins, *The Iron Age I Structure*, 53.

11. Hawkins cites Zertal, but also recognizes some debate. Hawkins, *The Iron Age I Structure*, 54–60.

12. Zertal notes the absence of sickle blades to be telling for determining the site's function. Zertal, "An Early Iron Age Cult Site," 148. Also, see Oded Borowski, *Agriculture*

perhaps more intriguing than any other site to date.[13] The sheer number was enormous. The remains of over 2800 bones were found, and 770 of them were identifiable. Ninety-six percent came from either cattle, sheep, goat, or fallow deer. Of the ninety-six percent, sixty-five percent were sheep and goat, twenty-one percent cattle, and ten percent deer. Over 120 bones were burnt, and twenty-five displayed cut marks. In the end, it's the nature and volume of the faunal remains that is trumpeted by many as important evidence for major cultic activity at the site.

There were also two Egyptian-style scarabs found at Ebal.[14] Scarabs are often considered index finds and thus highly valued. However, this does not mean that they are uncomplicated and automatically allow for precise dating. For example, the scarab designs of popular pharaohs may have been produced long after the pharaoh's death because of perceived apotropaic abilities. Regardless, it's definitive that the presence of a particular scarab signals the earliest point of existence.[15]

Scarab 1 (length 17.5mm x width 13mm x height 7.5 mm)[16] was found in Layer C of the fill dirt inside the large stone installation of Stratum I,[17] and Scarab II (length 14.25 mm x width 11 mm x height 6.5 mm)[18] was found in relationship to the many stone installations spattered through-out the site.[19] Both have been dated based on their iconographic similarity to other scarabs from around the globe to the final half of the thirteenth century.[20] Yet there has been significant debate on the precise dating of the scarabs, namely the suggestion that the founding of Stratum I should be in the twelfth century (vs. the end of the thirteenth).[21] Nevertheless, Hawkins

in Iron Age Israel (Boston: American Schools of Oriental Research, 2002; Repr., Winona Lake, IN: Eisenbrauns, 2009), 61–62.

13. L. K. Hurwitz, Faunal Remains from the Early Iron Age site on Mt. Ebal," TA 13–14 (1986–87): 173–89; N. Liphschitz, "Paelobotanical Remains from Mount Ebal," TA 13–14 (1986–87): 190–91, Also, Hawkins, The Iron Age I Structure, 63–66.

14. B. Brandl, "Two Scarabs and a Trapezoidal Seal from Mount Ebal," TA 13–14 (1986–1987): 166–72.

15. It's difficult to make a scarab before that person ever existed. See the discussion in Hawkins, The Iron Age I Structure, 66–67.

16. Brandl, "Two Scarabs," 166.

17. Hawkins, The Iron Age I Structure, 70–71.

18. Brandl, "Two Scarabs," 169.

19. Hawkins, The Iron Age I Structure, 71.

20. Brandl, "Two Scarabs," 166–70.

21. J. Weinstein, "Exodus and Archaeological Reality" in The Exodus: The Egyptian

argues that whatever side of the debate one falls the timeframe of potential usage is not significantly altered.[22] Consequently, Mt. Ebal was likely being used as a cultic site by the latter half of the thirteenth century, if not by the beginning of the twelfth century.

It should be noted that Zertal did not arrive at a cultic interpretation of the site all at once. Rather, it was apparently the result of a process that pivoted on a few important finds and conclusions. Zertal recalls that the most exciting element of el-Burnat, at least initially, was the pottery assemblage. The sheer volume of pottery and the nature of the assemblage, being characteristics of early Iron Age pottery, was fascinating.[23] Later, as the team excavated the large stone installation at the center of the site they noticed that there was no observable doorway into the structure, suggesting that some type of domicile was not likely.[24] Then there was the consideration of the site's location. It's essentially not near anything of strategic importance, including main roadway systems.[25] For Zertal this worked against any theory that saw the site in a militaristic vein. Yet Zertal claims that it was only when he thought of the structure from the vantage point of the fill did the pieces begin to fall into place in a meaningful way.[26] Zertal remembered Exod 27:8 with its stipulation that the tabernacle's altar was to be hallow. Thus, the installation at the center of the site, which exhibited no entry point, which was filled with ash and animal bones, and was essentially a hallow square, was actually a very, very large altar.

Eventually, Zertal went on to publicly ponder whether Joshua's altar had been found, which secured heavy criticism from virtually every direction. But to Zertal, the question was legitimate. In his mind, there was a cult site in the heart of the Central Highlands, on Mt. Ebal, with signs of cultic activity dating to the end of the thirteenth century or the beginning of the twelfth. So much of this reality matched passages in Deuteronomy (11:29; 27) and Joshua (8:30–35). But one of the dissenting voices was Aharon Kempinski.

Evidence (eds. E. S. Frerichs and L. H. Lesko; Winona Lake, IN: Eisenbrauns, 1997), 87–103.

22. Hawkins, *The Iron Age I Structure,* 70–71. Hawkins also cites Zertal's response via private correspondence.

23. Adam Zertal, "Has Joshua's Altar been found on Mt. Ebal?" *BAR* Jan/Feb (1985): 29.

24. Zertal, "Joshua's Altar," 30.

25. Zertal, "Joshua's Altar," 30.

26. Zertal, "Joshua's Altar," 35.

The Debate

Kempinski visited the site during the first year of Zertal's excavations. Subsequently, he developed an alternative interpretation of the site. Problematic for Kempinski were several elements observed on site. First, Kempinski references a fully intact collared rim store jar inside of what Zertal argued was the base of the altar. "One would hardly expect to find a whole storage jar inside an altar—if it were an altar!"[27] Moreover, Kempinski disagreed with Zertal's understanding of the fill inside the large stone installation. According to Kempinski, the fill is not indicative of a deliberately laid strata that bear witness to large-scale cultic activity. Rather, "the 'fill' inside the structure looked more like the normal debris or remains usually found after a building has been destroyed."[28]

According to Kempinski, the site on Mt. Ebal is better described as a three-phase village, a theory which purportedly finds support from other Iron Age I sites in the Central Highlands.[29] In the first phase, a semi-nomadic people group occupied the site with their tents and huts. This group left behind a vast array of pits and other small installations. The second phase saw a more stable settlement highlighted by the presence of multiple roomed homes as well as the construction of a generic enclosure. But between the second and third phases, Kempinski reconstructs a site-wide destruction. Out of the ashes of this destruction came a watchtower, the focal point of the third phase. Debris and other fill material were indiscriminately added to the central stone structure for its needed foundation.

27. Aharon Kempinski, "Joshua's Altar—An Iron Age Watchtower," *BAR* Jan/Feb (1986): 44.

28. Kempinski, "Joshua's Altar," 44; 48.

29. Kempinski, "Joshua's Altar," 44.

Kempinski also took issue with Zertal's ramp.[30] In Kempinski's mind, its narrowness prevented any use as a ramp. Rather, it should be understood as a wall, particularly since other well-known examples of other Iron Age cult sites prefer steps. As for the faunal remains, Kempinski interprets the data blandly—merely as the normal accumulation of sacrificial activity. And as if to land one final blow, Kempinski considers the Samaritan community and its Pentateuch. He questioned why Zertal did not consider the perspective of the Samaritan community, essentially implying that Zertal uncritically accepted the witness of the Masoretic Text over other textual traditions because it "fit" his data more effectively.

In turn, Zertal leveled a systematic response through a series of propositional statements.[31] First, Zertal claimed that several Kempinksi's assertions were deficient or just plain wrong. He highlighted the length of Kempinksi's stay—for one hour during the first year of excavation. Moreover, Zertal notes that Kempinski ignores Zertal's own admittance that his conclusion about Mt. Ebal is the result of a process that spanned several seasons of excavation and many hours of interpreting the totality of the data. Second, Zertal questions Kempinski's understanding and use of the data. For example, there is no observable destruction layer at the

30. Kempinski, "Joshua's Altar," 45.

31. Adam Zertal, "How Could Kempinski Be So Wrong!" *BAR* Jan/Feb (1986): 43; 49–52.

site, and so Kempinski's reconstruction of destruction between the second and third phases of the village misses the mark. Also, Zertal observes that Kempinski's theory fails to account for the copious small finds and precious metals that bolster a cultic interpretation for the site. Most importantly for Zertal, understanding el-Burnat as a watchtower is problematic because the site is geographically isolated.

With respect to Kempinski's understanding of the ramp and the witness of the Samaritan traditions, Zertal admitted that the discussion is hard. Zertal recognized that the terms used in discussions about altars and their architecture are often opaque. Yet he wondered if Ebal would clarify the discussion by providing material evidence to illuminate terms that are otherwise misunderstood. Regarding the Samaritan literary traditions, namely the Samaritan Pentateuch, Zertal found it hard to accept that the Samaritan textual traditions preserved the original text and that the Masoretic Text was a later corruption. Zertal pointed to the widespread agreement that the Samaritan Pentateuch shows deliberate alterations for ideological reasons. So, how could the Samaritan Pentateuch be a more reliable witness to the era of Joshua?

But Zertal had to deal with other detractors. For example, Volkmar Fritz and Patrick Miller both understood the remains at Ebal as evidence of farmstead, perhaps even a center of food production amid a large administration system centered in Shechem.[32] William Dever boldly wondered if the site was an Iron Age barbeque, a comment which he later clarified as factitious while remaining unconvinced.[33] Yet the problem with these alternative theories is the apparent lack of an entryway into the main structure, without which any sort of domicile is hard to imagine. And if the site is neither a domicile nor a cultic place, then is a militaristic site the most likely scenario?

Giloh, an Iron Age site near Jerusalem, can shed light of the situation. It's been interpreted as a militaristic site that included a watchtower. Consequently, it's a valuable comparative tool, particularly in light of Kempinski's ideas. Both Ebal and Giloh are only sparsely developed, show signs

32. Volkmar Fritz, *The City in Ancient Israel* (Sheffield: Sheffield Academic Press, 1995), 69–70; Robert Miller, *Chieftains of the Highland Clans: A History of Israel in the 12th and 11th Centuries BC* (Grand Rapids: William B. Eerdmans, 2005), 29–103.

33. William G. Dever, "How to Tell a Canaanite from an Israelite," in *The Rise of Ancient Israel* (ed. Hershel Shanks; Washington D. C.: Biblical Archaeological Society, 1992), 34; *idem, Who Were the Early Israelites and Where Did They Come From?* (Grand Rapids: William B. Eerdmans, 2003), 89–90.

of bordering that could be interpreted as a fortification, and exhibit a large central structure. However, Hawkins has noted a series of problems with parallels often invoked between Giloh and Ebal.[34] Namely, the Giloh site sits atop of its summit while the Ebal site does not. The main watchtower building at Giloh exhibits a solid base, which is neither exhibited at Ebal nor widely attested to until Iron II. Moreover, Ebal's wall is not formidable, it sits a significant distance from any major road or place of interest, and there is no associated fortification system nearby.

Admittedly, however, identifying a cultic site is notoriously difficult. This has been discussed by Michael Press.[35] Nevertheless, difficulty is not impossibility, and the critical factor is addressing the totality of evidence against a number of important considerations. For example, Ziony Zevit has offered fourteen considerations when evaluating a potential cultic site.[36] They include the following.

1. A place of natural significance

2. A place of historic significance

3. Actions performed there take place in an enclosed space

4. Architecture reflects the presence of ritual practice

5. Architecture reflects prayer and prescribed movements

6. Architecture identified places of importance

7. Evidence of cultic imagery and/or icons

8. The presence of sacred facilities

9. Evidence of sacrificial activity

10. Evidence of food and drink sacrifices

11. Presence of votive objects

12. Evidence of multiple attestation of symbols or structures

13. Architecture reveal evidence of an understanding of sanctity

14. Architecture reflects affluence

34. Hawkins, *The Iron Age I Structure,* 115–16.

35. Michael Press, "The Problem of Definition: 'Cultic' and 'Domestic' Contexts in Philistia," in *Household Archaeology in Ancient Israel and Beyond* (eds. Assaf Yasur-Landau; Jennie R. Ebeling, and Laura B. Marow; Leiden: Brill, 2011), 361–73.

36. Ziony Zevit, *Religions of Ancient Israel: A Parallactic Approach* (New York: Continuum, 2001), 82–84.

While the details of Zevit's catalog can be debated, it properly highlights a number of important issues: delineations of sacred space, evidence of sacrifice, the presence of votive offerings, religious ideals manifested in the site's architecture, and significance of the site, both natural or historical. Applied to Mt. Ebal, its height establishes it a place of natural significance, which is complimented by its historical significance (Deut 11; 27; Josh 8). The dynamics of the faunal remains and the high number of flint knives point to its status as a prominent center for sacrifice, and its architectural footprint can be interpreted as highlighting a central structure that appears to have been at the center of an idea of sacred space, perhaps even a series of sanctuaries (see below). In addition, the pottery assemblage, votive offerings, and drinking vessels suggest this to be a place where people brought offerings and libations. Consequently, the totality of the evidence suggests that the ruins toward the top of Mt. Ebal are likely those of a cultic center. If it walks like a duck, quacks like a duck, and looks like a duck, it's probably a duck.

The Implications of the Ruins on Mt. Ebal

Did Zertal find Joshua's altar? To answer this, one must first answer two other questions. First, does one accept a cultic function for the site? Second, does one accept the chronology of the site? In the case of the second question, there is little dispute, but the first question, as has been discussed, is the more difficult. Yet if one can answer both questions positively, then there is a high probability that the ruins on Mt. Ebal are associated with the site referenced in Deuteronomy and Joshua, although without any inscriptional verification one cannot be completely certain. Nevertheless, as just stated, I am convinced of its cultic function.

Proceeding from this, there are other implications than just the possibility that Zertal may have found Joshua's altar. First, the altar on Ebal may have been the original "place of the name." In 2007, Sandra Richter argued that the location so often discussed in Deuteronomy but never explicitly clarified—the place of Israel's central cult site—was Mt. Ebal.[37] According to Richter, the phrase in Deuteronomy *lešākkēn šēmō šām* is a loan-adapted form of the widely utilized Akkadian phrase *šuma šakānu*, which references the physical inscription of one's name, often through a

---

37. Sandra L. Richter, "The Place of the Name in Deuteronomy," *VT* 57 (2007): 342–66.

monument, to claim victory and lordship of that location.[38] Thus, when Deuteronomy describes the central cult site as the "place where the Lord will choose to put his name," it's suggesting that the site intends to remind Israel whom is their Lord. Indeed, the location of this central place is never explicitly detailed in Deuteronomy, but Richter argued through literary, literary-critical, topographical, and comparative angles that Deuteronomy does eventually inform the reader where the original place of the name was. "[I]t seems that the book does indeed answer the question is poses: the 'place of the name' within Deuteronomy is Mt. Ebal."[39]

Richter's argument is formidable, and Bill Arnold described it as "impressive."[40] Yet it has been challenged in conjunction with the fierce debate over Ebal in general. Nevertheless, Richter's previous work on the "place of the name" formula throughout the Old Testament's historical literature establishes a spectrum of development associated with the "place of the name." Therefore, it appears that what started at Ebal, eventually moved to Shiloh (cf. Jer 7:12) and then to Jerusalem.[41] In other words, it appears that at different points in Israel's history, different locations functioned as the central cult site uniquely positioned to nurture a governing theology critical to the nation's identity, an ideology that had at its core the notion that the Lord was Israel's conquering hero that deserved their undivided loyalty.

In another interesting argument, Ralph Hawkins ponders the relationship between Mt. Ebal and a series of "footprints," or "sandals," spread out across the Jordan Valley.[42] Hawkins points to a series of deliberately constructed enclosures made of unworked stone that generally resemble a large footprint. Each have been found to exhibit significant pottery assem-

---

38. See Richter's discussion, "The Place of the Name," 343–44. This work assumes her previously published monograph Sandra Richter, *The Deuteronomistic History and the Name Theology: lešakkēn šĕmô šām in the Bible and Ancient Near East* (BZAW 318; de Gruyter: Berlin, 2002).

39. Richter, The Place of the Name," 365.

40. Bill T. Arnold, "Deuteronomy as the *Ipsissima Vox* of Moses," *JTI* 4.1 (2010): 63–64.

41. The connection between these locations is a linguistic one. All of them are described as the place where the Lord "put his name," a description communicated by an idiom that takes one of two forms. Either it appears through the collaboration of שכן + שָׁם + שֵׁם or its related phrase שׂים + שֵׁם + שָׁם. For this linguistic relationship, see Richter's *The Deuteronomistic History and the Name Theology, passim.*

42. Ralph Hawkins, *How Israel Became a People* (Nashville: Abingdon Press, 2013), 179–87; *idem.* "Israelite Footprints," *BAR* March/April (2016): 44–49.

blages but no evidence of sustained settlement. Hawkins, in turn, considers whether these sites may have been constructed by semi-nomadic people during the same general timeframe of Israel's settlement. As to the function of such sites, Hawkins connects them to the various *gilgalim*, or Gilgals, mentioned in the Old Testament.[43] He also notes the cultic significance of these places, highlighting their role as places of circumcision and Passover celebration (Josh 5:2–11), covenantal renewal (Deut 11:30), and apostate worship (Hos 4:15; 9:15; 12:11; Amos 4:4–5; 5:5). In addition, Hawkins finds it significant that there were two massive footprints that highlighted the entrance of the temple at Ain Dara.[44]

According to Hawkins, the general shape of Ebal's enclosure walls recalls the shape of these *gilgalim*. Therefore, he connects the lot, eventually describing Mt. Ebal as the "westernmost" manifestation and linking them to Israel's western movement through the trans-Jordanian plateau into the Promised Land.[45] Together, these *gilgalim* show how altars played an important role for a people group as they moved to settle in a particular region.

Consequently, the significance of Mt. Ebal also exists in the discussion of how sanctuaries contributed to the construction of early Israelite identity. Indeed, Ebal offers an opportunity to understand how a specific find or site may (or may not) verify the general historicity behind the Old Testament. This is enough to get excited about. However, it's important to remember that archaeology does not set out to prove the Bible. It intends to unearth the cultural remains of a site so to understand more fully the dynamics of that site or the people that occupied that site. At Ebal, we see a site that apparently enjoyed a very prominent role in the cultic lives of the people who occupied the region, a role that also dissipated quickly.

Yet I suspect that the enduring quality of Ebal will be its witness to how worship and theology framed Israel's understanding of themselves and the Lord. In the early part of the twentieth century, Martin Noth put forth the idea that the twelve tribes of Israel were organized around cult sites, a reconstruction that owed its rationale to a comparison with the tribal leagues of Delphi and ancient Greece. However, after enjoying a few decades of prominence, the so-called Israelite Amphictyony was heavily criticized from multiple angles to the point where it is now largely rejected.[46] Nev-

43. Hawkins, *How Israel Became a People*, 182–84.

44. Hawkins, *How Israel Became a People*, 183; Hawkins, "Israelite Footprints," 49.

45. Hawkins, *How Israel Became a People*, 184.

46. For a synopsis of the debate, see A. G. Auld, "Amphictyony, Question of," in

ertheless, and with legitimate criticisms of the amphictyonite hypothesis notwithstanding, it may be time to revisit the role of central sanctuaries during the early stages of Israel's existence in the Central Highlands. The data at Ebal along with its implications have settled and, if Hawkins's assessment is correct, many scholars are more open to understanding the ruins of Mt. Ebal cultically.[47] And if it's site is accepted as a cultic site, its status as the original "place of the name" is not only more enticing but also enriching to further understanding the site and its communal significance. Many lines are converging, and it may be time to revisit some old ideas.

the *Dictionary of the Old Testament Historical Books* (eds. Bill T. Arnold and H. G. M. Williamson; Downers Grove, IL: InterVarsity, 2005), 26–32. Also, Hawkins, *The Iron Age I Structure*, 188–92.

47. Hawkins, *The Iron Age I Structure*, 198–99. The reasons for an ostensible shift are many, including advances in understanding politicalization processes in the ancient Near East.

Conclusion

The Old Testament is an anthology of texts that were not written in a vacuum. They were composed and preserved by a particular culture living in a particular time in a particular region of the world. Moreover, these texts preserve the experiences and understandings of that culture. Consequently, it stands to reason that fully understanding the content of the Old Testament requires an understanding of that culture. Therefore, archaeology is an indispensable tool for Old Testament studies, and Biblical Studies for that matter.

Yet archaeology is a discipline that must be respected. It certainly does not serve Biblical Studies—as if it exists solely to clarify the content of the Old or New Testaments. It has its own philosophies, its own intentions. It's concerned with analyzing material culture so that a better understanding of a people group of a certain place or region can be achieved. Sure, texts can be a part of the material culture left behind, but archaeology's concern is anthropological. However, with all this said, this work is convinced that archaeology will never be too far removed from Biblical Studies. If one takes seriously the notion that ancient Israel—its experiences and realizations about those experiences—are the chief vehicle for the revelation of Yahweh, then archaeology can never be completely removed from the picture nor conveniently ignored. Archaeology is uniquely positioned to tell us more about that culture and its world.

If there is one word that describes my current understanding of the relationship between archaeology and the Bible, it's "convergence." Inspired by William Dever, the results of archaeology at times converge with Biblical Studies. They are not parallel, as if they are perpetually existing side by side only to offer indirect illumination. Nor do they exist on top of each other, as if they must always speak directly to each other, positively or negatively.

143

Rather, the two disciplines have their own agendas and converge, enjoying points of contact where there is insight to be offered.

When these convergences happen, the nature of the cross-disciplinary discussion varies. At times, archaeology's contribution to Biblical Studies is more anthropological or conceptual. For example, the excavations at Mari have shown a light on institutions and realities associated with Israel's history and society. Ugarit yields information on the ever-critical Late Bronze Age and the Canaanite worldview, against which the Old Testament takes a vehement stand. And the Dead Sea Scrolls speak to the process of textual preservation, textual development, and Canonization. I have described these types of convergences as broad convergences, for such points of contact are not specific to any passage or topic but rather informative to an issue(s) that is broadly applicable across the Old Testament and/or the Bible.

At other times, archaeology converges in a very narrow way. The Ketef Hinnom amulets show how the general populace was using the priestly tradition in the last decades of the Judean monarchy. The Tel Dan Stele and the Taylor Prism attest to specific events in Israel and Judah's history and thus illuminate biblical history writing. In some instances, the convergence can be so narrow that certain historical realities of the biblical text can be verified, which seems to be the case with Mt. Ebal.

Yet in some special cases, the convergence can be both broad *and* narrow. The Gilgamesh Epic convergences in both broad and narrow ways. Its literary history offers insight in the scribal practices and mentalities behind the Canonization process of the Old Testament. Its content provides a window into the thought-world of ancient Near Eastern culture. Yet the Gilgamesh Epic also sounds strikingly similar to the biblical flood narrative, thereby making the Epic an indispensable comparative tool.

Consequently, one must concede that there is no simplistic or universal answer to the question, "What is archaeology's relationship to the Old Testament (or the Bible for that matter)?" The answer to such a question is unique to the situation in which it arises. As we have been discussing, sometimes the findings of archaeology are broadly applicable, but other times they are narrowly applicable. This means that every instance must be evaluated on a case-by-case basis. The debate is nuanced. And because it's nuanced, it's not wise to frame the discussion in binary terms, which has been the case in some circles. I am referring to the minimalist vs. maximalist debate that took place in recent memory, a debate that is still referenced today.[1] Generally, one was labeled a maximalist if you were perceived to positively affirm the relationship between archaeology and the Bible. That is, a maximalist saw archaeology as bolstering the historical claims and credibility of the Bible. By implication, the Bible is understood as a credible historical resource. Conversely, the label of minimalist was given to those who were perceived to possess a negative view on the issue. The minimalists questioned the historical claims of the Bible, often citing archaeological research, and ultimately sought to seriously question the integrity of the Bible as a credible historical resource. The reality is that archaeological research does both; it can affirm the witness of the Bible and encourage a critical evaluation of certain elements of the Bible's content. To put it in basic terms, archaeology can shine positively and negatively on the text. Therefore, it would be beneficial to jettison any scheme that frames the debate in a flat and unsophisticated fashion.

This minimalist vs. maximalist debate was put on vivid display beginning in 2007 when a group set out to excavate Khirbet Qeiyafa, a modest sized tel in the Israeli foothills. Excavations lasted until 2013, but what was produced in those few years set off a vigorous and robust debate that featured the so-called minimalists vs. the maximalists. One need to look no further than Yosef Garfinkel's "The Birth and Death of Biblical Minimalism" as proof.[2] Garfinkel argued that the excavations of Khirbet Qeiyafa presented the death blow to those who believe that the Old Testament does not display historical accuracy—only the ideological agendas of later periods. Whether this skepticism appears by denying the existence of David or Solomon, the United Monarchy, or radically adjusting the traditional chronology of the Iron Age, minimalists argue that the biblical text—at least for purposes of historical reconstruction—needs to be handled skeptically and delicately. Garfinkel argued that Qeiyafa must be associated with Judah and thus provides evidence of a capable centralized government in Judah during the early years of Iron II. By implication, Qeiyafa supports the picture created by the biblical text—that of a United Monarchy centered in Jerusalem.

Of course, such claims ensured passionate responses of those being targeted by Garfinkel's grand claims. Thus, in both academic and popular contexts, punches and counterpunches were thrown. At points, some

1. Dever is correct when he contextualizes this debate in the larger philosophical and intellectual debates that harnessed the pillars of post-modernity. See Dever, *What Did the Biblical Writers Know*, 23–52.

2. Yosef Garfinkel, "The Birth and Death of Biblical Minimalism," *BAR* 37.3 (2011): 46–53, 78.

accusations even called into question the competency of the other.[3] But the biggest problem with how the debate unfolded was that it created a false dichotomy in plain view of the public. Either you sided with the excavators and thus supported the historical veracity of the Bible. Or, you didn't, and therefore believed the Bible to contain gross historical fabrications. The reality, however, is that Finkelstein and Fantalkin are on target when they say, "The idea that a single, spectacular finding can reverse the course of modern research and save the literal reading of the biblical text regarding the history of Israel from critical scholarship is an old one."[4] It's difficult to see how the excavations at Khirbet Qeiyafa with its data published to date will "reverse the course of current research."

Nevertheless, Finklestein and Fantalkin understate the implications of Khirbet Qeiyafa when they frame any potential importance in terms of saving a "literal reading" from "critical scholarship." Both phrases are loaded terms and cannot be simplistically understood. And by throwing them around as Finkelstein and Fantalkin do, they lose any value, creating a false dichotomy that misses the mark in the process. Indeed, as I have stated, I don't think that the data of Khirbet Qeiyafa "dramatically changes the landscape of Biblical Studies."[5] Yet this is not to say that the finds at Khirbet Qeiyafa are not important. The site contributes greatly to a developing picture of the region during the Iron I/Iron II transition—whenever that took place.[6] Moreover, the contributions of Khirbet Qeiyafa allow the nuances of biblical history writing to be clarified. Consequently, because of Khirbet Qeiyafa scholars are reminded that reality exists behind biblical history writing while the conventions of the genre are thoroughly ancient and must be respected and evaluated as such. If this can be remembered, the claims of the biblical text can be more properly understood.

In terms of a convergence, Khirbet Qeiyafa represents a broad convergence. It does not speak to a specific passage or a specific issue, but it does inform our understanding of the transition between Iron I and Iron II. Khirbet Qeiyafa testifies to a region in flux where one socio-political

3. For example, Israel Finkelstein and Alexander Fantalkin, "Khirbet Qeiyafa; An unsensational Archaeological and Historical Interpretation," *TA* 39 (2012): 38–63.

4. Finkelstein and Fantalkin, "Khirbet Qeiyafa," 58.

5. David B. Schreiner, "What Are They Saying About Khirbet Qeiyafa," *TrinJ* 33NS (2012): 47.

6. For a good primer on this debate, see Israel Finkelstein and Amihai Mazar, *The Quest for the Historical Israel* (ed. Brian B. Schmidt; Atlanta: SBL Press, 2007), 107–39, esp. 118–23.

entity was beginning to exert itself into the territory beyond the Central Highlands. Yet it does not "prove" the United Monarchy to be an imperialistic entity ruling a geographic expanse from the border of Egypt to the western arm of the Euphrates. And it will certainly not silence adversaries of the Old Testament's general historical veracity. Nevertheless, as Khirbet Qeiyafa has a sophisticated relationship with the texts of 1 and 2 Samuel, archaeology will continue to have a sophisticated relationship with the Old Testament.

Bibliography

Abegg, Martin G. and Ben Zion Wacholder, eds. *A Preliminary Edition of the Unpublished Dead Sea Scrolls*. Washington, D. C.: Biblical Archaeology Society, 1991.

Ahituv, Samuel and Amihai Mazar. "The Inscriptions from Tel Rehov and their Contribution to the Study of Script and Writing during Iron Age IIA." Pages 39–68 in *"See I Will Bring a Scroll Recounting What Befell Me" (Is 40:8): Epigraphy and Daily Life from the Bible to the Talmud*. Edited by Esther Eshel and Yigal Levin. Göttingen: Vandenhoeck & Ruprecht, 2014.

Albright, W. F. *Archaeology and the Religion of Israel: The Ayers Lectures of the Colgate-Rochester Divinity School 1941*. Baltimore: Johns Hopkins, 1965.

Auld, A. G. "Amphictyony, Question of." Pages 26–32 in the *Dictionary of the Old Testament Historical Books*. Edited by Bill T. Arnold and H. G. M. Williamson. Downers Grove, IL: InterVarsity, 2005.

Angerstorfer, A. "Ašerah als 'consort of Jahwe' oder Aširtah?" *Biblische Notizen* 17 (1982): 7–16.

Athas, George. *The Tel Dan Inscription: A Reappraisal and a New Interpretation*. Journal for the Study of the Old Testament Supplements 360/Corpus inscriptionum semiticarium 12. Sheffield: Sheffield Academic Press, 2003.

Arnold, Bill T. "Deuteronomy as the *Ipsissima Vox* of Moses." *Journal of Theological Interpretation* 4.1 (2010): 53–74.

Barkay, Gabriel. "The Priestly Benediction on Silver Plaques from Ketef Hinnom in Jerusalem." *Tel Aviv* 19.2 (1992): 139–92.

Barkay, Gabriel, Andrew G. Vaughn, Marilyn J. Lundberg, and Bruce Zuckerman. "The Amulets from Ketef Hinnom: A New Edition and Evaluation." *Bulletin for the American Schools of Oriental Research* 334 (2004): 41–71.

Barkay, Gabriel, Marilyn J. Lundberg, Andrew G. Vaughn, Bruce Zuckerman, and Kenneth Zuckerman. "The Challenges of Ketef Hinnom: Using Advanced Technologies to Reclaim the Earliest Biblical Texts and their Context." *Near Eastern Archaeology* 66.4 (2003): 162–71.

Battenfield, James. "Archaeology." Pages 641–82 in *Old Testament Survey: The Message, Form, and Background of the Old Testament*. 2d Edition. Grand Rapids: William B. Eerdmans, 1996.

BEC Crew. "The Bible was Written Way Earlier then We Thought, Mathematicians Suggest." *Science Alert*, April 12, 2016. http://www.sciencealert.com/the-bible-was-written-way-earlier-than-we-thought-mathematicians-discover (accessed Jan 11, 2019).

Becking, Bob. "Did Jehu Write the Tel Dan Inscription?" *Scandinavian Journal of the Old Testament* 13 (1999): 187–201.

———. "The Second Danite Inscription Some Remarks." *Biblische Notizen* 81 (1996): 21–30.

Ben Zvi, Ehud. "On the Reading 'bytdwd' in the Aramaic Stele from Tel Dan." *Journal for the Study of the Old Testament* 64 (1994): 25–32.

Biran, Avraham and Joseph Naveh. "An Aramaic Stele Fragment from Tel Dan." *Israel Exploration Journal* 43.2–3 (1993): 81–98.

———. "The Tel Dan Inscription: A New Fragment." *Israel Exploration Journal* 45.1 (1995): 1–18.

Birot, Maurice. "Trois textes économiques de Mari (I)." *Revue d'assryiolgie et d'archéologie orientale* 47 (1953): 121–30.

———. "Textes économiques de Mari (II)." *Revue d'assryiolgie et d'archéologie orientale* 47 (1953): 161–74.

———. "Textes économiques de Mari (III)." *Revue d'assryiolgie et d'archéologie orientale* 49 (1955): 15–31.

———. "Textes économiques de Mari (IV)." *Revue d'assryiolgie et d'archéologie orientale* 50 (1956): 57–72.

Blenkinsopp, Joseph. *A History of Prophecy in Israel*. Revised and enlarged edition. Louisville: Westminster John Knox, 1996.

Bordreuil, Pierre and Dennis Pardee. *A Manual of Ugaritic*. Linguistic Studies in Ancient Western Semitic 3. Winona Lake, IN: Eisenbrauns, 2009.

———. "Ugarit: Texts and Literature." Pages 706–21 in Vol. 6 of the *Anchor Bible Dictionary*. Edited by David Noel Freedman. 6 vols. New York, Doubleday, 1992.

Borowski, Oded. *Agriculture in Iron Age Israel*. Boston: American Schools of Oriental Research, 2002; Reprinted Winona Lake, IN: Eisenbrauns, 2009.

Brandl, B. "Two Scarabs and a Trapezoidal Seal from Mount Ebal." *Tel Aviv* 13–14 (1986–1987): 166–72.

Bright, John. *A History of Israel*. 4h Edition. Louisville: Westminster John Knox, 2000.

Burrows, Millar. *The Dead Sea Scrolls of St. Mark's Monastery; Volume I: The Isaiah Manuscript and the Habakkuk Commentary*. New Haven, CT: American Schools of Oriental Research, 1951.

Cline, Eric H. *Biblical Archaeology: A Very Short Introduction*. Oxford: Oxford University Press, 2009.

———. *1177 B.C.: The Year Civilization Collapsed*. Princeton: Princeton University Press, 2014.

Craigie, Peter C. *Psalms 1–50*. Word Biblical Commentary 19. 2d Edition. Nashville: Thomas Nelson, 2004.

———. *Ugarit and the Old Testament*. Grand Rapids: William B. Eerdmans, 1983.

Cross, Frank Moore. "The Evolution of a Theory of Local Texts." Pages 306–20 in *Qumran and the History of the Biblical Text*. Edited by Frank Moore Cross and Shemaryahu Talmon. Cambridge: Harvard University Press, 1976.

———. "Notes on a Canaanite Psalm in the Old Testament." *Bulletin of the American Schools of Oriental Research* 117 (1950): 19–21.

Cryer, Frederick H. "On the Recently Discovered 'House of David' Inscription." *Scandinavian Journal of the Old Testament* 8 (1994): 3–20.

Currid, John D. *Doing Archaeology in the Land of the Bible: A Basic Guide*. Grand Rapids: Baker Books, 1999.

Dahood, Mitchell. *Psalms*. Anchor Bible Commentary 16. 3 Vols. Garden City, NJ: Double Day, 1966–70; Reprint Yale University Press, 1995.

Dalley, Stephanie. *Mari and Karana: Two Old Babylonian Cities*. 2d Edition. Piscataway, NJ: Gorgias Press, 2002.

Davies, P. R. "'House of David' Built on Sand: The Sins of the Biblical Maximizers." *Biblical Archaeological Review* 20.4 (1994): 54–55.

———. *In Search of "Ancient Israel."* Journal for the Study of the Old Testament Supplements 148. Sheffield: JSOT Press, 1992.

Day, John. "Asherah (Deity)." Pages 483–87 in Vol 1 of the *Anchor Bible Dictionary*. Edited by David Noel Freedman. 6 vols. New York, Doubleday, 1992.

———. "Baal (Deity)." Pages 545–49 in Vol 1 of the *Anchor Bible Dictionary*. Edited by David Noel Freedman. 6 vols. New York, Doubleday, 1992.

Dever, William. "A Critique of Biblical Archaeology: History and Interpretation." Pages 141–57 in *The Old Testament in Archaeology and History*. Edited by Jennie Ebeling, J. Edward Wright, Mark Elliot, and Paul V. M. Flesher. Waco: Baylor University Press, 2017.

———. *Did God Have a Wife? Archaeology and Folk Religion in Ancient Israel*. Grand Rapids: William B. Eerdmans, 2005.

———. "How to Tell a Canaanite from an Israelite." Pages 26–60 in *The Rise of Ancient Israel*. Edited by Hershel Shanks; Washington D. C.: Biblical Archaeological Society, 1992.

———. "The Impact of 'New Archaeology.'" Pages 337–52 in *Benchmarks in Time and Culture: Essays in Honor of Joseph A. Callaway*. Edited by J. F. Drinkard, Jr, G. L. Mattingly, and J. M. Miller. Atlanta: Scholars Press, 1988.

———. "The Impact of 'New Archaeology' on Syro-Palestinian Archaeology," *Bulletin of the American Schools of Oriental Research* 242 (1981): 15–29.

———. *The Lives of Ordinary People in Ancient Israel: Where Archaeology and the Bible Intersect*. Grand Rapids: William B. Eerdmans, 2012.

———. *What Did the Biblical Writers Know & When Did They Know It? What Archaeology Can Tell Us about the Reality of Ancient Israel*. Grand Rapids: William B. Eerdmans, 2001.

———. *Who Were the Early Israelites and Where Did They Come From?* Grand Rapids: William B. Eerdmans, 2003.

———. "Whom Do You Believe—The Bible or Archaeology?" *Biblical Archaeological Review*. 43.3 (May/June 2017): 43–47; 58.

Dietrich, Walter. "*dawid, dod,* und *bytdwd.*" *Theologische Zeitschrift* 53 (1997): 17–32.

Dijkstra, Meindert. "I have Blessed you by YHWH of Samaria and his Asherah: Texts with Religious Elements from the Soil Archive of Ancient Israel." Pages 17–44 in *Only One God? Monotheism in Ancient Israel and the Veneration of the Goddess Asherah*. Edited by Bob Becking, Meindert Dijkstra, Marjo C. A. Korpel, and Karel J. H. Vriezen. London: Sheffield Academic Press, 2001.

Dorsey, David A. *The Roads and Highways of Ancient Israel*. The ASOR Library of biblical and Near Eastern Archaeology. Baltimore: The Johns Hopkins University Press, 1991.

Durand, Jean-Marie. "Mari, (Texts)." Pages 529–36 in Vol. 4 of the *Anchor Bible Dictionary*. Edited by David Noel Freedman. 6 vols. New York, Doubleday, 1992.

Eisenman, Robert H. and James M. Robinson, eds. *A Facsimile Edition of the Dead Sea Scrolls*. 2 vols. Washington, D. C.: Biblical Archaeology Society, 1991.

Elayi, Josette. *Sennacherib, King of Assyria*. Atlanta: SBL Press, 2018.

Fagan, Brian D. *Return to Babylon: Travelers, Archaeologists, and Monuments in Mesopotamia*. Revised edition. Boulder, CO: The University Press of Colorado, 2007.

Faigenbaum-Golovin, Shira, Arie Shaus, Barak Sober, David Levin, Nadav Na'aman, Benjamin Sass, Eli Turkel, Eli Piasetzky, and Israel Finkelstein. "Algorithmic Handwriting Analysis of Judah's Military Correspondence Sheds Light on Composition of Biblical Texts." *Proceedings of the National Academies of Sciences* 117.17 (2016): 4664–4669.

Feldt, Laura. "Religion, Nature, and Ambiguous Space in Ancient Mesopotamia: The Mountain Wilderness in Old Babylonian Religious Narratives." *Numen* 63 (2015): 1–36

Finkelstein, Israel and Alexander Fantalkin, "Khirbet Qeiyafa; An unsensational Archaeological and Historical Interpretation." *Tel Aviv* 39 (2012): 38–63.

Finkelstein, Israel and Amihai Mazar, *The Quest for the Historical Israel*. Edited by Brian B. Schmidt. Atlanta: SBL Press, 2007.

Fishbane, Michael. *Biblical Interpretation in Ancient Israel*. Oxford: Clarendon Press, 1988.

Fleming, Daniel. "The Amorites." Pages 1–30 in *The World Around the Old Testament: The People and Places of the Ancient Near East*. Edited by Bill T. Arnold and Brent Strawn. Grand Rapids: Baker Academic, 2016.

———. *Democracy's Ancient Ancestors: Mari and Early Collective Government*. Cambridge: Cambridge University Press, 2004.

Freedman, David and J. C. Geoghegan. "'House of David' is There!" *Biblical Archaeology Review* 21.1 (1995): 78.

Fritz, Volkmar. *The City in Ancient Israel*. Sheffield: Sheffield Academic Press, 1995.

Galil, Gershon. "A Re-arrangement of the Fragments of the Tel Dan Inscription and the Relations between Israel and Aram." *Palestine Exploration Quarterly* 133 (2001): 16–21.

Garfinkel, Yosef. "The Birth and Death of Biblical Minimalism," *Biblical Archaeology Review* 37.3 (2011): 46–53, 78.

George, A. R. *The Babylonian Gilgamesh Epic: Introduction, Critical Edition, and Cuneiform Texts*. 2 Vols. Oxford: Oxford University Press, 2003.

Ginsberg, Harold L. "A Phoenician Hymn in the Psalter." Pages 472–76 in *Atti del XIX Congresso Internazionale degli Orientalisti*. Rome: Tipografia del Senato, 1938.

Gmirkin, Russel. "Tool Slippage and the Tel Dan Inscription." *Scandinavian Journal of the Old Testament* 16 (2002): 293–302.

Gogel, Sandra L. *A Grammar of Epigraphic Hebrew*. SBL Resources for Biblical Studies 23. Atlanta: The Society of Biblical Literature, 1998.

Govier, Gordon. "Ancient Sticky Notes Shift Secular Scholars Closer to Evangelicals on Bible's Age." *Christianity Today*, under "News." http://www.christianitytoday.com/ct/2016/april-web-only/ancient-sticky-notes-shift-secular-scholars-older-bible.html (accessed Jan 11, 2019).

Grayson, A. K. and Jamie Novotny. *The Royal Inscriptions of Sennacherib, King of Assyria (704-681 BE), Part 1*. Winona Lake, IN: Eisenbrauns, 2012.

Hadley, Judith M. "Some Drawings and Inscriptions on Two Pithoi from Kuntillet Ajrud." *Vetus Testamentum* 37.2 (1987): 180–213.

Hagelia, Hallvard. *The Dan Debate: The Tel Dan Inscription in Recent Research*. Recent Research in Biblical Studies 4. Sheffield: Sheffield Phoenix Press, 2009.

Hallo, William W, ed. *The Context of Scripture*. 3 Vols. Leiden. Brill, 2003.

Hallote, Rachel. " 'Bible Lands Archaeology' and 'Biblical Archaeology' in the Nineteenth and Early Twentieth Centuries." Pages 111–39 in *The Old Testament in Archaeology and History*. Edited by Jennie Ebling, J. Edward Wright, Mark Elliot, and Paul V. M. Flesher. Waco: Baylor University Press, 2017.

Halpern, Baruch. *David's Secret Demons: Messiah, Murderer, Traitor, King*. Grand Rapids: William B. Eerdmans, 2001.

———. "The Stela from Dan: Epigraphic and Historical Considerations." *Bulletin of the American Schools of Oriental Research* 296 (1994): 63–80.

Harrison, R.K. "Archaeology and the Bible." Pages 156–60 in *Baker Encyclopedia of the Bible*. Edited by Walter A. Elwell and Barry J. Beitzel. Grand Rapids: Baker Book House, 1988.

Hawkins, Ralph K. "Biblical Archaeology" in *The Lexham Bible Dictionary*. Edited by John D. Barry. Bellingham, WA: Lexham Press, 2016. Logos Bible Software.

———. *How Israel Became a People*. Nashville: Abingdon Press, 2013.

———. *The Iron Age I Structure on Mt. Ebal: Excavation and Interpretation*. Winona Lake, IN: Eisenbrauns, 2012.

———. "Israelite Footprints." *Biblical Archaeology Review* March/April (2016): 44–49.

———. *Joshua*. Evangelical Critical Commentary. Bellingham, WA: Lexham Press, forthcoming.

Hays, Christopher B. *Hidden Riches: A Sourcebook for the Comparative Study of the Hebrew Bible and Ancient Near East*. Louisville: Westminster John Knox, 2014.

Heimpel, Wolfgang. *Letters to the King of Mari: A New Translation, with Historical Introduction, Notes, and Commentary*. Mesopotamian Civilizations. Winona Lake, IN: Eisenbrauns, 2003.

Heiser, Michael. "What's Ugaritic Got to Do with Anything?" *Logos Bible Software*, https://www.logos.com/ugaritic (accessed on January 1, 2019).

Hess, Richard. "Asherah or Asheratah?" *Orientalia* 65 (1996): 209–19.

———. *Israelite Religions: An Archaeological and Biblical Survey*. Grand Rapids: Baker Academic, 2007.

Hurwitz, L. K. "Faunal Remains from the Early Iron Age site on Mt. Ebal." *Tel Aviv* 13–14 (1986–87): 173–89.

Keck, Brian E. "Mari (Bibliography)." Pages 536–38 in Vol. 4 of the *Anchor Bible Dictionary*. Edited by David Noel Freedman. 6 vols. New York, Doubleday, 1992.

Kempinski, Aharon "Joshua's Altar—An Iron Age Watchtower." *Biblical Archaeology Review* Jan/Feb (1986): 42; 44–49.

Kitchen, Kenneth. "A Possible Mention of David in the Late Tenth Century BCE, and Deity *Dod as Dead as the Dodo?" *Journal for the Study of the Old Testament* 76 (1997): 29–44.

Kottsieper, Ingo. "Die Inschrift vom Tell Dan und die politischen Beziehungen zwischen Aram-Damaskus und Israel in der 1. Hälfte des 1. Jahrtausends vor Christus." Pages in 475–500 *"Und Mose schrieb dieses Lied auf": Studien zum Alten Testament und zum Alten Orient. Festschrift für Oswald Loretz zur Vollendung seines 70. Lebensjahres mit Beiträgen von Freunden, Schülern un Kollegen. Unter Mitwirkung von Hanspeter Schaudig*. Alter Orient und Altes Testament 250. Münster: Ugarit-Verlag, 1998.

Knauf, Ernst Axel, D. de Pury, and Thomas Römer. "*Baytdawid ou *Baytdod? Une relecture de la nouvelle inscription de Tel Dan." *Biblische Notizen* 72 (1994): 60–69.

Knott, Elizabeth. "A Review of Jean-Claude Margueron, *Mari, Capital of Northern Mesopotamia in the Third Millennium: The archaeology of Tell Hariri on the Euphrates*." *Near Eastern Archaeology* (2016): 36–42

Kriwaczek, Paul. *Babylon: Mesopotamia and the Birth of Civilization*. New York: Thomas Dunne Books, 2010.

Kuhrt, Amélie. *The Ancient Near East: c. 3000–330 BC*. Routledge History of the Ancient World. New York: Routledge, 1995.

Lemaire, André. *Les écoles et la formation de Bible dans l'ancien Israel*. Orbus Biblicus et Orientalis 39. Freibourg: Editions Universitaires; Göttingen: Vandenhoeck & Ruprecht, 1981.

———. "'House of David' Restored in the Moabite Inscription." *Biblical Archaeological Review* 20.3 (1994): 30–37

———. "The Tel Dan Stele as a Piece of Royal Historiography." *Journal for the Study of the Old Testament* 81 (1998): 3–14.

Lemche, Niels and T. L. Thompson. "Did Biran Kill David? The Bible in Light of Archaeology." *Journal for the Study of the Old Testament* 64 (1994): 3–22.

Lemche, Neils. "Bemerkungen über einen Paradigmenwechsel aus Anlaß einer neuentdeckten Inschrift." Pages 99–108 in *Meilenstein Festgabe für Herbert Donner zum 16. February 1995*. Edited by M. Weippert and S. Timm. Ägypten und Altes Testament 30. Wiesbaden: Otto Harrassowitz, 1995.

Liphschitz, N. "Paelobotanical Remains from Mount Ebal." *Tel Aviv* 13–14 (1986–87): 190–91.

Lupinski, E. *The Arameans: Their Ancient History, Culture, Religion*. Orientalia Lovaniensia Analecta 100. Leuven: Peeters, 2000.

Magness, Jodi. *The Archaeology of Qumran and the Dead Sea Scrolls*. Grand Rapids: William B. Eerdmans, 2002.

Malamat, Abraham. *Mari and the Bible*. Vetus Testamentum Supplements 12. Ledien: Brill, 1998.

———. *Mari and the Early Israelite Experience*. The Schweich Lectures of 1984. Oxford: Oxford University Press, 1989.

Matthews, Victor H. "The West's Rediscovery of the Holy Land." Pages 83–110 in *The Old Testament in Archaeology and History*. Edited by Jennie Ebling, J. Edward Wright, Mark Elliot, and Paul V. M. Flesher. Waco: Baylor University Press, 2017.

Margueron, Jean-Claude. "Mari (Archaeology)." Pages 525–29 in Vol. 4 of the *Anchor Bible Dictionary*. Edited by David Noel Freedman. 6 Vols. New York: Doubleday, 1992.

———. *Mari, Capital of Northern Mesopotamia in the Third Millennium: The archaeology of Tell Hariri on the Euphrates*. Oxford: Oxbow Books, 2014.

Mazar, Amihai. *Archaeology of the Land of the Bible: 10000–586 BCE*. The Anchor Bible Reference Library. New York: Doubleday, 1990.

Mazar, Amihai and Nava Panitz-Cohen. "It is the Land of Honey: Beekeeping at Tel Rehov." *Near Eastern Archaeology* 70.4 (2007): 202-19.

Meshel, Ze'ev. "Kuntillet Ajrud." Pages 103–09 in Vol. 4 of the *Anchor Bible Dictionary*. Edited by David Noel Freedman. 6 Vols. New York: Doubleday, 1992.

Millard, Alan. "Absence of Word Divider Proves Nothing." *Biblical Archaeology Review* 20.6 (1994): 68–69.

Miller, Patrick D. *The Religion of Ancient Israel*. Library of Ancient Israel. Louisville: Westminster John Knox, 2000.

Miller, Robert. *Chieftains of the Highland Clans: A History of Israel in the 12th and 11th Centuries BC*. Grand Rapids: William B. Eerdmans, 2005.

Mitchell, Chris and Julie Stahl, "Have Archaeologists Found Prophet Elisha's House?" *Christian Broadcasting Network*. Embedded Video File, 4:04. http://www.cbn.com/cbnnews/insideisrael/2013/july/have-archaeologists-found-prophet-elishas-house/?mobile=false (accessed Jan 11, 2019).

de Moor, J. C. *The Seasonal Pattern in the Ugaritic Myth of Ba'lu*. Alter Orient und Altes Testament 16. Neukirchen: Vluyn, 1971.

Moorey, P. R. *A Century of Biblical Archaeology*. Louisville: Westminster John Knox, 1991.

Moss, Candida. "Does this Handwriting Prove the Bible's Age?" *The Daily Beast*. http://www.thedailybeast.com/articles/2016/04/12/does-this-ancient-handwriting-prove-the-bible-s-age.html (accessed Jan 11, 2019).

Na'aman, Nadav. "Beth-David in the Aramaic Stele from Tel Dan." *Biblische Notizen* 79 (1995): 17–24.

Noth, Martin. *The Deuteronomistic History*. Journal for the Study of the Old Testament Supplements 15. Sheffield: JSOT Press, 1991.

Ortiz, Steven. "Archaeology, Syro-Palestinian" Pages 60–79 in *Dictionary of the Old Testament Historical Books*. Edited by Bill Arnold and Hugh Williamson. Downers Grove, IL: InterVarsity Press, 2005.

Pallis, Sven. *The Antiquity of Iraq: A Handbook of Assyriology*. Copenhagen: Ejnar Munksgaard, 1956.

Pitard, Wayne T. "Before Israel: Syria-Palestine in the Bronze Ages." Pages 25–57 in *The Oxford History of the Biblical World*. Edited by Michael D. Coogan. Oxford: Oxford University Press, 1998.

Press, Michael. "The Problem of Definition: 'Cultic' and 'Domestic' Contexts in Philistia." Pages 361-89 in *Household Archaeology in Ancient Israel and Beyond*. Edited by Assaf Yasur-Landau, Jennie R. Ebeling, and Laura B. Marow. Leiden: Brill, 2011.

Rainey, Anson. "The 'House of David' and the House of the Deconstructionists." *Biblical Archaeological Review* 20.6 (1994): 47.

Rasmussen, Carl G. *Zondervan Atlas of the Bible*. Revised edition. Grand Rapids: Zondervan, 2010.

Rasovsky, Marina, David Bigelajzen, and Dodo Shenhav. "Cleaning and Unrolling the Silver Plaques." *Tel Aviv* 19.2 (1992): 192–94.

Rensburg, Gary A. "On the Writing bytdwd in the Aramaic Inscription from Tel Dan." *Israel Exploration Journal* 45 (1995): 22–25.

Renz, Johannes. *Handbuch der althebräschen Epigraphik*. 3 Vols. Darmstadt: Wissenschafliche Buchgesellschaft, 1995.

Richter, Sandra L. *The Deuteronomistic History and the Name Theology: lešākkēn šēmō šām in the Bible and Ancient Near East*. Beihefte zur Zeitschrift für die alttestamentliche Wissenschaft 318. de Gruyter: Berlin, 2002.

———. "The Place of the Name in Deuteronomy." *Vetus Testamentum* 57 (2007): 342–66.

Robinson, E. and E. Smith. *Biblical Researches in Palestine, and in the Adjacent Regions*. 2 Vols. Boston: Crocker and Brewster, 1856–1860.

Rollston, Christopher. *Writing and Literacy in the World of Ancient Israel: Epigraphic Evidence from the Iron Age*. Society of Biblical Literature: Archaeology and Biblical Studies 11. Atlanta: Society of Biblical Literature, 2010.

Romey, Kristin. "Discovery of Philistine Cemetery may Solve Biblical Mystery." *National Geographic*. July 10, 2016. https://news.nationalgeographic.com/2016/07/bible-philistine-israelite-israel-ashkelon-discovery-burial-archaeology-sea-peoples/ (accessed January 25, 2019).

Sáenz-Badillos, Angel. *A History of the Hebrew Language.* Translated by John Elwolde. Cambridge: Cambridge University Press, 1993.

Sasson, Jack M. *From the Mari Archives: An Anthology of Old Babylonian Letters.* Winona Lake, IN: Eisenbrauns, 2015.

———. "The King and I: A Mari King in Changing Perceptions" *Journal for the American Oriental Society* 118 (1998): 453–70.

Schmid, Konard. *Genesis and the Moses Story: Israel's Dual Origins in the Hebrew Bible.* Translated by James D. Nogalski. Siphrut 3. Winona Lake, IN: Eisenbrauns, 2010.

Schmidt, Brian B. "The Iron Age Pithoi Drawings from Horvat Teman or Kuntillet Ajrud: Some New Proposals." *Journal of Ancient Near Eastern Religions* 2 (2002): 91–125.

Schniedewind, William M. *How the Bible Became a Book.* Cambridge: Cambridge University, 2004.

———. "Tel Dan Stela: New Light on Aramaic and Jehu's Revolt." *Bulletin of the American Sschools of Oriental Research* 302 (1996): 75–90.

Schreiner, David B. "Potsherds, Computers, and the Composition of the Bible." Wesley Biblical Seminary, entry posted April 14, 2016. http://www.wbs.edu/2016/04/ potsherds (accessed Jan 11, 2019).

———. "What Are They Saying About Khirbet Qeiyafa," *Trinity Journal* 33NS (2012): 33–48.

———. "Wilderness, Theology of " in the *Global Wesleyan Dictionary of Biblical Theology.* Edited by Robert Branson, Sarah Derck, Deirdre Brower Latz, and Wayne McCown. Kansas City: The Foundry Publishing, forthcoming.

Shanks, Hershel, ed. "Biblical Minimalists Meet their Challengers Face to Face." *Biblical Archaeology Review* 23.4 (1997): 26–42; 66.

———. "Is this Man a Biblical Archaeologist? BAR Interviews William Dever—Part One." *Biblical Archaeology Review* 22.4 (1996): 30-39; 62-63.

———. "Is this Man a Biblical Archaeologist? BAR Interviews William Dever—Part Two," *Biblical Archaeology Review* 22.5 (1996): 31-37; 74-77.

———. "Three Shekels for the Lord: Ancient Inscription Records Gift to Solomon's Temple." *Biblical Archaeology Review* 23.6 (1997): 28–32.

Smoak, Jeremy D. "May Yhwh Bless You and Keep You from Evil: The Rhetorical Argument of Ketef Hinnom Amulet I and the Form of the Prayers for Deliverance in the Psalms." *Journal of Ancient Near Eastern Religions* 12 (2012): 202–36.

Soulen, Richard N. and R. Kendall Soulen. *Handbook of Biblical Criticism.* 3d Edition. Louisville: Westminster John Knox, 2001.

St. Fleur, Nicholas. "Story of Philistines Could be Reshaped by Ancient Cemetery." *New York Times,* July 10, 2016 under "Science." http://www.nytimes.com/2016/07/11/ science/possible-philistine-cemetery-discovered.html?smprod=nytcore-iphone&smid=nytcore-iphone-share (accessed Jan 11, 2019).

Sparks, Kenton L. *Ancient Texts for the Study of the Hebrew Bible: A Guide to the Background Literature.* Peabody, MA: Hendrickson Publishers, 2005.

Stern, Ephraim. *Archaeology of the Land of the Bible: Volume II.* The Anchor Bible Reference Library. New York: Doubleday, 2001.

Thompson, T. L. *Early History of the Israelite People.* Studies in the History of the Ancient Near East 4. Leiden: Brill, 1992.

Tigay, Jeffrey. *The Evolution of the Gilgamesh Epic.* Wauconda, IL: Bolchazy-Carducci Publishers, Inc., 2002.

Tov, Emanuel. *Textual Criticism of the Hebrew Bible.* Second and revised edition. Minneapolis: Fortress Press, 2001.

Ussishkin, David. *The Renewed Archaeological Excavations at Lachish (1973–1994), Volumes I–V.* Monographs of the Institute OF Archaeology 22. Tel Aviv: Tel Aviv University, 2004.

VanderKam, James. *The Dead Sea Scrolls Today.* Grand Rapids: William B. Eerdmans, 1994.

van der Toorn, Karel. *Scribal Culture and the Making of the Hebrew Bible.* Cambridge: Harvard University Press, 2007.

Waaler, Erik. "A Revised Date for Pentateuchal Texts?: Evidence from Ketef Hinnom." *Tyndale Bulletin* 53.1 (2002): 29–54.

Wade, Nicolas. "Modern Technology Unlocks Secrets of Damaged Biblical Scroll," *New York Times,* Sept 21, 2016 under "Science." http://www.nytimes.com/2016/09/22/science/ancient-sea-scrolls-bible.html?_r=0 (accessed Jan 11, 2019).

Waltke, Bruce and Michael O'Connor. *An Introduction to Biblical Hebrew Syntax.* Winona Lake, IN: Eisenbrauns, 1990.

Walton, John and Brent Sandy. *The Lost World of Scripture: Ancient Literary Culture and Biblical Authority.* Downers Grove, IL: IVP Academic, 2013.

Weinstein, J. "Exodus and Archaeological Reality" Pages 8–103 in *The Exodus: The Egyptian Evidence.* Edited by E. S. Frerichs and L. H. Lesko. Winona Lake, IN: Eisenbrauns, 1997.

Wesselius, Jan-Wim. "The First Royal Inscription from Ancient Israel: The Tel Dan Inscription Reconsidered." *Scandinavian Journal of the Old Testament* 13 (1999): 163–86.

———. "The Road to Jezreel: Primary History and the Tel Dan Inscription." *Scandinavian Journal of the Old Testament* 15 (2001): 83–103.

Wilford, John Noble. "Monopoly Over Dead Sea Scrolls is Ended," *New York Times,* Sept 22, 1991. https://www.nytimes.com/1991/09/22/us/monopoly-over-dead-sea-scrolls-is-ended.html (accessed on Jan 8, 2019).

Williams, Michael. *Basics of Ancient Ugaritic: A Concise Grammar, Workbook, and Lexicon.* Grand Rapids: Zondervan, 2012.

Wise, Michael, Martin Abegg, Jr., and Edward Cook. *The Dead Sea Scrolls: A New Translation.* New York: HarperCollins, 2005.

Wyatt, Nicolas. "Asherah." Pages 99–105 in the *Dictionary of Deities and Demons in the Bible.* Edited by Karel van der Toorn, Bob Becking, and Pieter Willem van der Horst. Leiden/Boston/Köln/Grand Rapids; Cambridge/Brill/William B. Eerdmans, 1999.

———. *Religious Texts from Ugarit.* 2d Edition. Sheffield: Sheffield Academic Press, 2002.

Yardeni, Ada. "Remarks on the Priestly Blessing on Two Amulets from Jerusalem." *Vetus Testamentum* 41.2 (1991): 176–85.

Yamauchi, Edwin. "Archaeology." Pages 148–56 in *Baker Encyclopedia of the Bible.* Edited by Walter A. Elwell and Barry J. Beitzel. Grand Rapids: Baker Book House, 1988.

Yon, Margeurite. *The City of Ugarit at Tell Ras Shamra.* Winona Lake, IN: Eisenbrauns, 2006.

Young, Robb Andrew. *Hezekiah in History and Tradition.* Vetus Testamentum Supplements 155. Leiden: Brill, 2012.

Younger, Jr., Kyle Lawson. "Aram and the Arameans." Pages 229–66 in *The World around the Old Testament*. Edited by Bill T. Arnold and Brent A. Strawn. Grand Rapids: Baker Academic, 2016.

Zertal, Adam. "An Early Iron Age Cult Site on Mount Ebal: Excavation Seasons 1982–1987; Preliminary Report," *Tel Aviv* 13–14 (1986–87): 105–65.

———. "Ebal, Mount (Place)." Pages 255–58 in Vol. 2 of the *Anchor Bible Dictionary*. Edited by David Noel Freedman. 6 Vols. New York: Doubleday, 1992.

———. "Has Joshua's Altar been found on Mt. Ebal?" *Biblical Archaeology Review* Jan/Feb (1985): 26–43.

———. "How Could Kempinski Be So Wrong!" *Biblical Archaeology Review* Jan/Feb (1986): 43; 49–52.

Zevit, Ziony. *The Religions of Ancient Israel: A Parallactic Approach*. New York: Continuum, 2001.

Lightning Source UK Ltd.
Milton Keynes UK
UKHW021333050819
347427UK00011B/2599/P